You Can Win Souls

You
Can Win Souls

C. E. Autrey

BROADMAN PRESS
Nashville, Tennessee

To the memory of
my beloved father
E. A. AUTREY, SR.

Foreword

Several years ago it was my privilege to attend a deeply spiritual state evangelistic conference. The church building was so filled with people that I could not find even a place to stand; therefore, I made my way to an adjoining building, in which a loud speaker had been placed for those who thus shared in the overflow service. Waiting there, listening over the public address system, I heard for the first time the voice of a flaming minister whom I did not know and whom I had never seen. The tone of his voice, the earnestness of his message, and the clear-cut presentation of his appeal made a profound impression upon me. That was my first time to hear Dr. C. E. Autrey, and that evening was my first time to meet the man of God face to face. From that hour until this present moment I have followed his career with increasing interest and with immeasurable gratitude for his devotion to the cause and message of soul-winning.

This volume is the result of his long years of pastoral and pedagogical and preaching ministries. Out of a full life he writes concerning this all-important subject of evangelism, and the chapters by which he presents his message are most practical, most complete, and most blessed. He not only speaks of the theory and the doctrinal basis for the work of evangelism, but he illustrates in a most powerful way the great truth that

v

he presents. In this volume we actually learn how to deal with the anxious seeker, the tragically deceived, the hopelessly indifferent, and almost every other type of individual that the consistent soul-winner will inevitably meet. Here are Scripture passages to use; here are approaches to be made; here are explanations to be presented; and here are methods to bring the lost soul to a definite and saving decision in Christ. Blessed is the student in the class and blessed is the preacher in the study and blessed is the layman in his work who reads these enlightening and inspiring pages.

All of us desperately need help in this mightiest of all God-given commissions, that of making disciples. The assignment of the Holy Spirit is one of soul-winning. The first task of the church is that of soul-winning. The first impulse of a born-again Christian is to win somebody to Jesus. If we lose this drive, we are untrue to the Holy Spirit within us and we deny the great will of God for us. Any book on evangelism that is faithful to the Scriptures is a book that is desperately needed; how much more so is this marvelous volume, written by a dedicated and able evangelist-pastor-teacher.

It is my humble persuasion that God will bless and sanctify the message of this volume beyond most other books on evangelism that have ever been written. In the classroom, in the pastor's study, and in the hearts of all who take time to learn its message, it will be a veritable fountain of strength and inspiration. Dr. Autrey as pastor, Dr. Autrey as teacher, and Dr. Autrey as evangelist has been wonderfully blessed of God. Dr. Autrey as author will be no less blessed in this marvelous volume.

W. A. CRISWELL

CONTENTS

Chapter 1

The Urgency of Individual Evangelism

I just needed someone to drag me out. All along I knew that my family and I needed to attend church and to know Christ as our Saviour. During the last two years I have thought often of our need of Christ, but I could not bring myself to start to church. I just needed someone to come along and drag me out." These words were spoken by a man who had joined the church on profession of faith at the morning service. A team of soul-winners had gone to his home the day before and had led him, his wife, and two teen-age children to trust Christ. He had been aware of his need long before the team visited him. He wanted to do something about it, but he did not and very likely never would have if someone had not gone into his home and confronted him with the claims of Christ. Being brought face to face with his spiritual condition gave the needed incentive.

The words of this man should haunt us and challenge us to go out in search of many thousands who are in similar condition. They may be remotely interested, but they are so preoccupied with things that without a personal touch they will never come to Christ. This family and thousands like it constitute the main reason for individual evangelism.

1

The Definition of Individual Evangelism

Individual evangelism is confronting the lost personally with the gospel of Christ. It is urging the lost to accept Christ as Saviour. Individual evangelism may be done over the telephone, by letter, or face to face. It is far more effective and fruitful when done face to face.

The Reasons for Individual Evangelism

Personal evangelism is scriptural. Personal evangelism is implied in the Old Testament in the magnificent drama of the twenty-fourth chapter of Genesis, but personal evangelism is specifically set forth in many places in the New Testament. The first two disciples came to Christ as a result of the personal testimony of John the Baptist (John 1:35–37). Jesus won Nicodemus, the ruler of the Jews, with a personal interview (John 3). In the fourth chapter of John, Jesus went out of his way to deal with the sinful woman. He went across the currents of popular opinion and established customs. His love for all humanity and his burning desire to see them come to God thrust him forth as an individual evangelist.

Jesus taught his disciples to do individual evangelism. He often sent them out by twos from house to house to bear witness and to prepare the way for his coming that he might more completely lead them to a knowledge of God.

Individual evangelism was employed by the apostle Paul. When Paul and Barnabas had gone through the island of Cyprus and came to Paphos, they found a certain sorcerer, a false prophet, a Jew whose name was Bar-Jesus. Bar-Jesus was a personal adviser of the proconsul, Sergius Paulus. Paul was so effective in personal evangelism that he was able to win Sergius Paulus to a knowledge of Christ in spite of the hindrances of Elymas, the sorcerer (Acts 13:6–13).

When Paul was thrown into prison in Philippi for preaching the gospel of Christ in public, he won the jailer to a saving knowledge of Christ. Later in his writing Paul gave emphasis to personal evangelism. He exhorted the Philippians to strive "together for the faith of the gospel" (Phil. 1:27). Paul told the Philippians that they were to strive together in the faith by their conversation. The burden of sin and the joy of release in Christ were to permeate their conversation. He added, "Holding forth the word of life" (Phil. 2:16). The lifeline of the early disciples was individual evangelism. They could continue to advance only as long as they personally held forth the word of life. This great principle was recognized by the apostle Paul and sponsored by him.

This method of personal evangelism was the major technique of the early church. When the Christians were scattered, Philip and many like him went out from place to place, telling about the power of Christ to save. Philip led the Ethiopian chancellor to Christ. Peter led the Roman centurion in Caesarea to Christ. Great crowds were inevitable as the mighty cause of Christ gathered momentum, and on major occasions mass conversions were witnessed. Simultaneously, however, the disciples used the less spectacular method as they dealt with lost individuals.

They literally "gossiped" the good news as they were scattered over the earth. The New Testament account says, "Now they which were scattered abroad upon the persecution . . . travelled as far as Phenice, and Cyprus, and Antioch, preaching the word to none but unto the Jews only" (Acts 11:19). The word for preach here is the word *laleō*, which literally means "to talk" and could be translated "to gossip." They talked it over the back fence, under olive trees, at the wells of water, and they shouted it on the streets. Gossip is used by Satan to slander character and curb great movements. The early disciples used gossip to hinder Satan and to advance the kingdom of righteousness. Every Christian should tirelessly "gossip" the good news. Let the good news clear the air of bad news. Bad news disconcerts and spreads fear, while good news soothes the nerves and makes glad the soul.

Dr. A. C. Archibald has reminded us that in first-century Christianity the burden was upon the man in the pew, but a few centuries later, when the Catholic perversion came, the emphasis was transferred to the "man at the altar." [1]

Personal evangelism is the hope of our age. The nation whose people are ignorant of God is in danger of disaster. "Sin is a reproach to any people" (Prov. 14:34). Sin destroyed Judah in the sixth century before Christ. Rebellion against God destroyed the beautiful Babylonian civilization. Sin like metal-teethed termites ate the iron out of the foundation of the Roman Empire in a later century. Sin threatens America and the whole world now. Revival of spiritual religion would do great good just as revivals have always helped in the past, but we must see in this generation an army of men and women who will not be detoured from entering every home and every phase of life with a personal appeal for repentance.

Our modern cities are mighty wildernesses of ignorance. The inhabitants have become preoccupied with making a livelihood. They either have a false conception of the churches or none at all. They must be dealt with personally. They will not be reached any other way. They, for the most part, feel lonely and unloved. They are convinced that no one really cares about their problems. They struggle desperately in a sea of selfishness. They feel that anyone who approaches them about anything must have some ulterior motive. A warm, genuine concern would surprise them. This concern could be demonstrated only in individual evangelism.

Individual evangelism is the hope of the world because it is the only way to reach the great masses of lost people. Ninety-seven per cent of the unchurched and unsaved never attend any kind of church. Only 3 per cent of the lost population of this country ever enter the doors of a church. The bulk of great sermons which are built at the expense of time and energy and delivered faithfully by the great preachers of the world are delivered for the most part to about 3 per cent of the lost population of the world. It is imperative, therefore, that we fall upon a method that will give our message to more people.

The most popular and publicized evangelists do not draw many lost people to hear them. The vast crowds which heard Billy Sunday, Dwight L. Moody, and those who hear our beloved Billy Graham today are largely church members. The unchurched have never gone to public religious meetings in great numbers to hear the gospel. The deluded and misinformed do not hear our sermons. The only way to reach them is through individual evangelism.

The one-by-one method of evangelism is God's prime method.[2] One cannot reach a hundred unless he can reach one. The most effective witnessing in the world is witnessing to the individual. If the world is ever brought to Christ, it will be done by the one-by-one technique. Men accept or reject Christ individually. Even though a man is converted in a great mass meeting, it is still an individual experience. Great preaching has always had its place; but the most urgent need at home and abroad is not for a great pulpit ministry, but for preachers who can and will talk effectively with men heart to heart and one at a time about the Saviour. The writer has labored in the Far East, the Near East, Europe, and all over America, and he has found that the prime need is for soul-winners. The foreign fields do not need great preachers, but they need men dedicated to the one-by-one method of evangelism.

Dwight L. Moody was a great pulpit evangelist, but he gave more concern to the number of individual souls he could reach personally than to preaching before great audiences. He regarded his pulpit appeal only as preparatory. To him, pleading with individual souls in the inquiry room was of more importance than his appeal before the great audiences.[3] It is said that Mr. Moody knelt by, pleaded with, prayed for, and won personally seven hundred fifty thousand people to Christ during his busy lifetime.[4] He could hardly wait until his appeal was over to retire to the inquiry room and help win wounded souls. When one realizes how popular Mr. Moody was as a preacher and how much time he gave to building a great institution of education, it is hard to believe that he could have found time enough to win so many to Christ personally. it would have been impossible except for the hunger in his heart and his dedication to the most prolific method of evangelism, namely, individual evangelism.

Our religious leaders are beginning to realize the need of individual evangelism. The need for personal evangelism was seen clearly by Dr. L. R. Scarborough as he pressed the claims of Christ in *With Christ After the Lost*. Dr. C. E. Matthews, secretary of evangelism of the Home Mission Board for many years, stressed the importance of individual evangelism when he took an account of the need of it to every church in his convention. The report of a commission on evangelism appointed by the Archbishops of Canterbury and York in 1945 expresses a deep concern for the same need. The report says in part:

The ministry of evangelism is a charge laid upon the whole church of the Lord. It is the very essence of the Christian calling . . . the evangelism of England . . . is a work that cannot be done by the clergy alone. It can be done to a small extent by the clergy at all. There can be no wide-spread evangelism of England unless the work is undertaken by the people of the church.[5]

It is encouraging that the leaders of many evangelical denominations are becoming more and more conscious of the need of individual evangelism, but the masses of Christians are not as yet aware of the importance of it. There is a universal awareness of the need of evangelism in general among the masses of Christians, but the need for personal evangelism has not yet been recognized. The truth remains that every real child of God was originally imbued with the spirit and desire to win. If that urge has died out of the individual Christian, then the church should re-examine its methods and purpose. Every Christian will continue to feel the urge and will follow it if properly taught and directed by his church.

Personal evangelism is our responsibility. The apostle Paul recognized this truth and gave expression to it when he said, "For necessity is laid upon me" (1 Cor. 9:16). In the parable of the talents in the twenty-fifth chapter of Matthew, Jesus is teaching among other things that any church whose members are not interested in winning the lost forfeits its rights to exist. Jesus called men from every walk of life. He called the lowly fishermen and said unto them, "Follow me, and I will make you fishers of men." He taught them by example and by precept to catch men for God. Their purpose in following him was to become soul-winners (John 15:27). At the end of his ministry, he commanded them to teach their followers all the things which he had taught them (Matt. 28:20).

As long as there is one person on any island or continent who has not heard the gospel, no Christian will be relieved of his great responsibility. Every time I look at the sun in the heavens it reminds me of my solemn task. That ball of fire in its haste across the heavens tells me that every time it sets in the west it closes the last chapter for thousands of doomed lives. Of all the thousands around the world who die daily, the majority of them are without knowledge of Christ.

Individual evangelism may be done in any situation. The wise soul-winner will always pray and look for a chance to bear witness for Christ. On a crowded bus an old Christian woman sat between two men who were busily reading the paper. She prayed for a chance to speak a word for Christ to one of them. If one is concerned enough, he will pray; and if he prays, God will open the door for testimony. Presently she looked over at one of the men and said, "They didn't get all the news in the paper this morning." The man became very interested. In fact, he became more interested in what they did not get into the papers than in the eighteen pages of news he held in his hand. He replied, "Well, what did they leave out?" She then answered, "The best news of all, that Christ died to save sinners." Then quickly and diplomatically she talked to him about his soul. If one cares enough for an opening to speak to the lost, God will give him a chance, and almost any situation can be transformed into a proper atmosphere for witnessing for Christ.

Old John Vasser, a native of Poughkeepsie, New York, was a great soul-winner. He did individual evangelism in the homes, on the streets, in the army, in hotel lobbies, on trains, and wherever the opportunity presented itself. One day he saw a lady sitting in the lobby of a hotel and walked up to her and asked her the pointed, personal question, "Are you a Christian?" She became very interested and with rapt attention listened to what the soul-winner had to say. When her husband returned, she told him how a perfect stranger had asked her the question, "Are you a Christian?" Her husband replied, "I suppose you told him it wasn't any of his business." She answered her husband, "No, I did not answer him thus because if you had been here to see the expression on his face and to hear him ask the question, you would have known it was his business." When the witness is dedicated to God and in the hands of the Spirit of God, he will operate in such an atmosphere as to transform any situation into a soul-winning opportunity.

Personal evangelism is our greatest work. It is the basis of all our religious work. It is not merely a booster for the rest of our work, but it is the very lifeblood of it. History fails to record a single great awakening that was not preceded and accompanied by vigorous, personal soul-winning. All else we may do gathers its inspiration and strength from individual evangelism.

Southern Baptists have a small hospital located high up in the mountains of Gilead, just outside Ajloun. It is an oasis in a desert of suffering and spiritual blindness. Dr. John Roper and other doctors and nurses connected with him consistently bear witness to Christ as they minister to the physical ills of the highlanders. As Dr. and Mrs. Roper took me over the rugged roads to the ancient city of Jerash, I had opportunity to talk at length with them (Mrs. Roper is a medical doctor also). I asked them: "Why did you come away out here to serve? Doctors are in great demand back in America. You could do fine back home financially and otherwise as well as heal the sick. Why do you remain in this wilderness?" Their answer revealed one thing— dedication to soul-winning. Soul-winning was their prime purpose in being in Jordan, and healing bodies was secondary. Individual evangelism gives meaning and purpose to everything we do, whether it be in connection with an educational institution, a hospital, or a church.

The condition of lost souls makes personal evangelism imperative. The condition of the sinner is set forth by the expression of the apostle Paul, "For the wages of sin is death" (Rom. 6:23). Sin damns. Sin destroys. Sin is not a mistake. Sin is a disease that destroys. Sin is an inner condition of the soul. Sin is a transgression of the law. The picture of sin and its terrorism over the lost soul should be a challenge to the soul-winner.

Leonardo da Vinci painted a picture of the face of a beautiful child. He became so fascinated by the picture that he placed it in his studio where he could constantly gaze upon it. The face of the lovely child tranquilized his soul in sorrow and in anger. He resolved in later life to paint a picture which would be its opposite. Long and patiently he searched for a model. He looked for a person whose features had been so scarred by sin that the face would be the opposite of the features of the beautiful child. After giving up the search, one day by accident he looked upon the almost inhuman face of a criminal on the floor of a prison cell. He had found the model he had been looking for. After gaining permission, he painted the hideous face. Then he learned to his utter amazement that the crime-hardened man and the angelic child were one and the same. Sin had transformed the angel into a demon. Sin had marred, disfigured, and destroyed.[6]

Individual evangelism can be done by any sincere person

who has been saved and who loves lost souls. He may not at first know much about methods, but his earnestness will suffice until he has learned more through study and experience. It requires no extraordinary talents, nor does it require an extra amount of education.[7] Ordinary laymen can do individual evangelism as effectively as anyone if they exercise sane judgment and tact.

Any man who can operate a grocery store, sell insurance, or gather laundry can learn to win souls. A man who operates a laundry truck must know how to gain entrance to the homes, how to conduct himself in the homes, and how to win the confidence of the prospective customers. These things are essential if he is to sell the services of the laundry. If the soul-winner believes in the Christ whom he represents and knows how to get the attention of a lost man and win his personal confidence, he should be able to introduce his Master to the prospect. It is a simple operation that requires concern, love, patience, tact, and a prayerful consciousness of the presence of God.

The task is so urgent that we cannot wait until we have attained to start. A young lawyer pleads before the bar for the life of an innocent client and loses. His heart is crushed, and he is tempted to quit, but when he faces reality, he knows he cannot change his profession. He will work harder the next time. He must speak for those who do not know how to plead their own case. The saved individual cannot wait until he has matured and become thoroughly taught. He must plead the cause of Christ the best he can in the courts of human hearts. He must help those who are not even aware of their doom. He must labor in ignorance, in tears, in earnest, in willing eagerness for the souls of eternity-bound men.

Chapter 2

The Qualifications
of the Soul-Winner

An effective salesman will have certain necessary characteristics. A successful executive will possess some fundamental qualities which others do not possess. The soul-winner will be characterized by the proper spiritual condition. His attitude and relation to Christ will be reflected in these qualities. We shall discuss a few of the most prominent qualities of the soul-winner. We admit that many Christians do not possess these qualities, but they are attainable by every child of God.

The soul-winner must be converted. The master soul-winner said, "Ye must be born again" (John 3:7). An experiential knowledge of Christ is imperative in soul-winning.

This experience with Christ produces within one a new life. Vital Christianity is a spiritual contagion. If one really has the life of God in him, others can catch it from him. He will by nature spread the influence and effect. You can catch the measles only from one who has the disease. Those who have Christ in their hearts can expose others to a knowledge of Christ.

Experiential knowledge of Christ will create a longing to see others saved.[1] The inner urge to bring others to Christ is essen-

11

tial to effective evangelism. The church must enlist its members in soul-winning classes and teach and urge them to confront men for Christ, but unless there is a longing from within, they will never become effective witnesses. A great knowledge of techniques does not produce a soul-winner. It will greatly enhance his efforts if he possesses the divine drive from within. Pastors and churches cannot produce this inner longing. It is the work of God in conversion. This urge will die, however, unless the churches take up from there with a continuous program of teaching and promotion.

Experiential knowledge of Christ furnishes one with a road map of the way to God. Jesus declared this in answer to the question of Thomas concerning his relation to God the Father. Jesus said, "I am the way, . . . no man cometh unto the Father, but by me" (John 14:6). No one can guide you through the forest who has not traveled the path before. No one can describe and point the way to God who has never traveled the road himself. Church members who have never experienced Christ as Saviour may ask others to unite with the church, but they will never try to lead them to Christ as Saviour. They do not know to do it, and they do not know the way.

No one whose knowledge is limited to what he has read in books can instruct others in the art of flying a plane. He must fly many hours before he can instruct others. No man can instruct others in how to come to Christ unless he has himself traveled over the path to Christ.

John Wesley is an example of the point under consideration. He was a fine, religious young man. He lived a noble life while in Oxford, and while a student in Oxford he engaged often in religious debate. He gathered around him a group of young men of pure motives who fasted, prayed, preached in jails and to the underprivileged. He even went to America as a missionary to the Indians. However, it was not until after his Aldersgate experience that he became a soul-winner and one of the most effective evangelists and churchmen of all time. He wrote in his diary, "I, who went to America to convert the Indians, have never myself been converted to God." [2]

The soul-winner's life must be above reproach. This does not mean that he must be perfect but that his life must be clean. He must be a living example of the fruits of his gospel. He must live all that he preaches and more. If his life is not clean, the lost will say, "Physician, heal thyself." A sickly salesman could never sell vitamin pills under the caption that they will "make one strong and vivacious." Prospective customers would ask, "Why have not these pills made you healthy and virile?" Verbal arguments will have no effect apart from a changed life. Andrew's words would never have affected blunt, stubborn Simon Peter if something else had not been present. Andrew's words were dynamic and challenging. He said, "We have found the Messias, which is, being interpreted, the Christ" (John 1:41). These words would have been startling and provocative to almost any Jew, but the glee in Andrew's voice and the sparkle in his eye and the changed disposition captured Simon. Simon followed Andrew to Jesus because he sensed a radical transformation in his brother. The change in Andrew, and not his words, laid hold on Simon.

The nameless prostitute met Jesus at Jacob's well, and was so radically changed that she left her waterpot and went back into the city of Nablus and simply said, "Come, see a man, which told me all things that ever I did: is not this the Christ?" (John 4:29). Her words were so simple, but the citizens who knew her as a sordid woman of the streets saw a change in her which amazed them. The city followed her outside to the well and heard Jesus, and many believed. A changed life in itself is not enough, but it is a basic essential. One must be like Christ to bring men to Christ.

In his writings to Timothy Paul often referred to the proper conduct of the man of God. He warned young Timothy to "take heed unto thyself" (1 Tim. 4:16). The soul-winner must have no black marks upon his character. Hearers will not respond to the appeals of one in whom they have no confidence. The evangelist must be right with God before he goes forth to witness. The witness who is guilty of known sin cannot preach the whole gospel. Jesus saves his people from their sins (Matt. 1:21). If a man is not saved from his sins, he cannot promise that the gospel he preaches will do more for others than it has done for him. The most facile speaker whose life harbors sin will be less effective than a blundering, clumsy talker who speaks from a clean heart. A Christlike character is a disarming argument for the reality of Christ. There is no answer to the argument of a pure life.[3]

A soul-winner must be a vessel unto honor. A clean vessel is imperative in witnessing for God (2 Tim. 2:21). No man is responsible for the size or the kind of vessel he is. God made him and determined his capacity, but man is accountable for being clean. You may be a small earthen vessel, but you can be clean. Spurgeon reminds us that no wise dairyman would pour milk into filthy bottles.[4] Likewise, God would not honor instruments that would reflect on his character. The Word of God is vital in the salvation of sinners. God's Word is powerful. God spoke, and all creation came into being. "God said, Let there be light: and there was light" (Gen. 1:3). The spoken or written word can produce life. Jesus stood before the grave of Lazarus and said, "Lazarus, come forth" (John 11:43), and the dead man arose. If men are to live spiritually, the Word of God must be used. God will not pour his Word through unclean vessels. Any witness who would use the Bible with power must be clean in heart and life.

God will not attend the ministry of an impure servant. It is disastrous enough to be shorn of power in the use of God's Word, but, what is worse, God's Spirit will not be with an unclean person in any effort. One who ceases to be holy in his living may continue to work for God out of habit, but he will be impotent. God is not with him. God said of the false preachers in the time of the revival under Hezekiah, "I sent them not, nor commanded them: therefore they shall not profit this people at all" (Jer. 23:32). The tongue of the soul-winner which is not under God's direction will sound empty and will in no case profit the people.

The evangelist who has been shorn of his power is sure to lay the blame on the people. He will fuss at the church. He will condemn the age in which he lives as being the worst of all time. His charges may be true, but this is not the reason for evangelistic failure. The greatest revivals in history have come out of times of spiritual dearth. The main fault lies with the evangelist. The reason for failure is always found in the heart of the evangelist and not in the condition of the age.[5] If the soul-winner will repent of sins, clean up his life, and humble himself before God, the presence of God will attend him and victory will ensue.

Charles Grandison Finney died at the age of eighty-three, but he remained an effective evangelist until the time of his death. For half a century God used him to keep the gales of evangelism fresh up and down the Atlantic seaboard. Often Mr. Finney would go out to conduct a revival, and the revival would bog down. The crowds would come, but nothing particularly would happen. He would always recognize that the reason for this was lack of power. Although he did not compromise with sin and often condemned sin wherever he found it, he did not lay the blame for lack of power on the people. He would always go away, get on his knees, and confess all the known sins in his life and any sin that he might have committed of which he had no knowledge; and he continued to confess them until God forgave him. Then the power would come back, and the revival would move on. This is one reason that Mr. Finney was so effective in evangelism for such a long period of time. He kept his heart clean. He realized that the danger to the soul-winner is generally from within.

The soul-winner must be spiritually minded. Paul exhorted the Roman believers, "And be not conformed to this world: but be ye transformed by the renewing of your mind, that ye may prove what is that good, and acceptable, and perfect, will of God" (Rom. 12:2). Paul was impressing on them the need for consecration of mind and life to God. They were not to fashion their thinking after the non-Christian society. If they modeled their thinking after the pagans, they would soon indulge in the corrupt practices of the pagans. "For as he thinketh in his heart, so is he." The believers were urged to model their lives after the will of God and not the trends of the age.

How could a Christian rise above the customs and styles of his age? Simply by being transformed through the renewing of his mind. To be transformed means to be transfigured. The word "transfigured" comes from the word "metamorphosis." This is what happens to the ugly silkworm when it wraps itself in a cocoon and remains for a while and then cuts its way out and emerges a beautiful silkfly. It is transfigured. We have all seen homely features made attractive by a glow which stems from a renewed mind. When one falls in love, there come a sparkle to the eye and a glow on the face that cannot be hidden. When one's mind has been renewed through Christ, it will be reflected in the facial expressions and demonstrated in all future decisions.

The renewed mind is the basis of consecration.

Consecration involves first a dedication. When one is consecrated, he is set apart to a definite task. Certain things are "off-beat" to him. This is the negative aspect, but far more important are the positive features of consecration.

Consecration means, literally, to fill the hands. When a person walks down the street with a load that fills his hands so completely that there is no space for anything else, it can be said of him that he is consecrated at that moment to that task. When a life is so occupied with God and the things of God that there is no room for anything else, it is consecrated.

One's consecration is seen in the point of his interest. The bootblack looks only at the shoes of the passer-by. He observes them closely to see if they need a shine in order that he might beckon to the man to stop by for service. That is his business. He is dedicated to that. The barber will not look at a man's shoes. He is not interested particularly in whether he has a shine or not. He will look at his hair and will observe the amount of hair, the kind of hair, and the style. That is his business. That is the thing to which he is consecrated. The third man will not observe the shoes or take even a glance at the hair but will observe the eyes. He will notice in a glance if the individual wears glasses, and if so, what kind. He is an optometrist. He is consecrated to helping men obtain better vision. The soul-winner will long to know the condition of the soul of everyone he meets. He will not concern himself with the financial standing, the amount of education which the individual possesses, but his concern will be with the soul.

It is essential that he be properly orientated in the Christian life. He must know where he stands before God. He knows that he is a child of God. He knows why he is a believer. He knows that he can trust the Holy Spirit to guide him. He need never be dogmatic, but he should be firm and well settled in his convictions. The devil often assailed the faith of the writer as a young preacher. He tried to lead me to doubt. He would say: "You are not really saved. Here you are trying to tell others how to become Christians, and you yourself have never been converted."

One day while I was preaching in a revival in my hometown, he put forth a special effort to strangle me with doubts. I walked out into a wooded section in back of the house where it was my honor to be guest. I wrestled with God in prayer. At that minute God gave me the victory through a single passage of Scripture. God reminded me that the answer to my struggle with doubts was in the Bible. There blazed into my mind like neon letters of fire, "All that the Father giveth me shall come to me: and him that cometh to me I will in no wise cast out" (John 6:37). I told the Lord earnestly: "I have come to you. I have come in repentance and simple trust. I have come the only way you have taught men to come to you. You said, 'Him that cometh to me I will in no wise cast out.' I have taken you at your word. I have come believing that under no circumstance would you refuse me, and from here on my salvation no longer depends on me but upon you and your word."

Victory over doubt came that instant. I took John 6:37 and whipped Satan mercilessly with it, until his attacks were fewer and fewer. My faith is in the Word of God and not in logic or feelings. The words of Christ are the last words of authority in earth and in heaven. When the writer walks up to the gates of heaven, if Peter or if angel Gabriel is standing there and inquires, "By what rights do you expect to enter?" I shall reply, "By the words of Christ," and I shall quote John 6:37. At these authoritative words of Christ, Gabriel, with every hair of his head ablaze with the glory and power of God, will bow politely and say, "Enter in, for the words of Christ the Lord are the last words of authority here."

Doubts usually come from one of three sources.

Idleness is one of the main sources of doubt, and an idle Christian is in grave danger. If he is not busy doing positive things for righteousness, his mind will become the devil's workshop. The child of God should fear idleness as he would a deadly contagion.

Known sin in one's life breeds doubt. If one knows that he is guilty of sin, soon he will begin to doubt his salvation and even God's power to save. Sin is the greatest source of doubt.

Ignorance breeds doubt. If one is ignorant of the Bible and the nature of God, he becomes fertile ground for the seeds of doubt. A well-rounded knowledge of revealed truth is a shield from doubt. A knowledge of the gospel establishes one in the truth that he has been saved from the sins of the past. It teaches him that he is being saved from the power of present sins and temptations and that one day he will be saved from the very presence of sin.

The soul-winner must be a willing follower of Christ. A Christian may serve all of his life in his hometown, but he must be willing to go anywhere should God lead him. If he is called to lands afar, he must go without hesitation. To refuse to obey God is to get completely out of his will. If God leaves him in his own hometown, he must work there as faithfully as if he were working in some foreign land. It is often more difficult to witness in one's hometown than it is in foreign lands. When Jesus had finished speaking by the lake of Gennesaret, he commanded his disciples to launch out and let down their nets for a catch. Simon reminded him that they had fished all night in these very waters and had taken nothing. Then Simon made a significant statement: "Nevertheless at thy word I will let down the net" (Luke 5:5). They enclosed a large number of fish. They fished at the command of Jesus, and they fished where he suggested.

If God lays a foreign land on one's heart, no matter where it is, he has no choice but to obey. "Woe unto him that striveth with his Maker!" (Isa. 45:9). Jonah learned this lesson the hard way. His rebellion brought forth the anger of nature. The tempest and the ocean combined to thwart his plans of rebellion. The disobedient servant will feel the combined strength of all forces against him. On the other hand, the obedient servant will feel the combined strength of all forces back of him. When the kings of Jerusalem, Hebron, Jarmuth, Lachish, and Eglon came up against the city of Gibeon and Joshua's forces, God sent a discomforting hailstorm, which assisted mightily in the defeat of the league of kings (Josh. 10:11). The stars will fight in their courses for the man who is dedicated to the will of God. The stars may not fight and the hail may not fall until the willing servants have thrown themselves without reserve into the fray.

The soul-winner must possess a passion for the lost. The effective witness will have an earnest desire to see souls converted. Without a burning desire the soul-winner will be detoured from his main job. Scores of other worthy causes will eclipse the main work. Unconsciously, the witness will be turned aside to a task of less magnitude unless the inner drive of compassion repeatedly impels him onward. This passion for the lost must overshadow every other desire.

It must be stronger than the desire to live. John Knox had it when he cried, "Give me Scotland or I die." It must take precedence over one's desire for community or national prominence. Moses offered himself as a sacrifice of oblivion for his sinning brethren. His passion for their condemned souls was so great that he prayed that his name be blotted out of the records along with them if God could not forgive their sins (Ex. 32:32). Paul's passion for his brethren took precedence over his eternal soul. He confessed, "I could wish that myself were accursed from Christ for my brethren, my kinsmen according to the flesh" (Rom. 9:3).

John Knox remade his nation. Moses saw a mighty revival which inscribed the name of his people in the records of God. Paul witnessed the conversion of many of his brethren and the establishment of great churches. The labors of these men were fruitful basically because of their passion for their people.

A burning passion produces a warm heart. Jesus stood on the slopes of the Mount of Olives and looked at the city of Jerusalem and wept. She was the city of the prophets, the religious capital of the world. She stood so close to the heart of God and so near salvation, yet so far away. She was blind and lost. Tears must have flowed copiously down his cheeks as he said, "If thou hadst known . . . in this . . . day, the things which belong unto thy peace! but now they are hid from thine eyes" (Luke 19:42). He saw more than the city of Jerusalem in that look. He looked down the vista of time and saw our generation, and his great heart swelled with consuming passion. He wept for us. We must know this passion if we are to win souls.

A driving passion stems from love. The only enduring motive is love. If the concern of the witness comes from genuine love, it will be irresistible. People of all classes and backgrounds, however uneducated and uncouth, are quick to detect sincerity. Sincerity stands out wherever it exists. All people admire earnestness. One who really loves will be sincere, courageous, patient, and effective. Dr. Torrey says, "There is nothing so irresistible as love." [6] It was a driving passion which caused John Wesley to ride horseback over indescribably bad roads a distance of nine times around the world.

The love of God manifested in one's life not only sends him out to labor for Christ, but it draws men to the gospel. Every heart hungers for love. Men will submit themselves to the most rigorous hardships and intimidations for love. The church which demonstrates its love for people by its actions and spirit will have more people flocking to it than it can serve.

One cold Sunday morning in Chicago, with frost upon the ground, a small, thinly dressed boy made his way toward the Moody Memorial Church. He stopped in a filling station to warm his toes. The attendant asked him, "Where are you going?" He replied, "To the Moody Memorial Church." "Where do you live?" he was asked. When he told where he lived, the attendant said: "You have already passed a dozen churches, and you will pass at least another dozen churches before arriving at the Moody Memorial Church. Why do you pass by them to go all the way to that church?" The child replied, "Because they love little boys like me down there at that church."

It is necessary that the effective witness be aware of the place of the Holy Spirit in his life. Dr. J. C. Macaulay has pointed out that the soul-winner needs the Holy Spirit to lead him.[7] Being led by the Holy Spirit is a mark of sonship, "For as many as are led by the Spirit of God, they are the sons of God" (Rom. 8:14). The Holy Spirit prepares us for witnessing, and he prepares the unconverted for our testimony.

One Saturday night the writer went out visiting the lost. When I arrived at the door for the first visit, there was no light in the building. I took it that no one was there and excused myself with a feeling of relief and drove away without ever stopping to ring the doorbell. The Spirit bore down upon me as I drove away and convicted me for failing to make sure whether the occupants were at home or not. So intense was the conviction that I returned and knocked on the door. I was happily surprised when the lady of the house turned on the porch light and opened the door. She and her husband were both at home, and they invited me to come in. They were ready for the visit of a man of God. Both of them were converted that night and came to join the church the next day.

The leading of the Spirit made possible the visit and gave the results. All of us, on the other hand, have made visits in which the Holy Spirit had no part. He needs us to work at both ends of the line. The leadership of the Holy Spirit is essential.

Every evangelist has experienced the difficulty of deciding which invitation to accept for a revival effort. After long hours in prayer he knows without a doubt which door he must pass through. When he has been on the scene for a few days, he will understand why the Holy Spirit led him to that particular place. People with anxious faces will come by to tell him how God used him to answer their grave problems. Homes will be saved from the rocks and souls snatched as firebrands from the burning by his brief ministry. All the while the Holy Spirit knew that the particular type of preaching and ministry which only he could do was needed at that special time in that community. If the evangelist had been motivated by a desire to preach to larger crowds or to preach for a more wealthy congregation, he would have missed the chief joy of an evangelist. The evangelist must be led only and always by the Holy Spirit.

The soul-winner needs the ability that only the Holy Spirit can provide. One may possess great clarity of thought and the weight of logic. He may be eloquent in conversation and cultured in approach; and these things are to be desired, but not substituted for divine unction. The ability provided by the Holy Spirit is an attribute of God. It is never the ability of the soul-winner. He is the conductor of the power. It flows through him like electricity flows through a wire. The wire does not possess the electricity. The electricity merely flows through the wire. This power is possessed as long as the Holy Spirit is operative in the life.

For a long time Mr. Moody preached with slightly above average results. One day the Holy Spirit was given his place in Moody's life. His power flooded Moody's soul. After that, when he preached the same simple sermons, the results were amazing. The sermons were the same, but great conviction resulted and large numbers responded because a new power was present. The breath of the Holy Spirit made the difference. Charles Finney was filled with the power of the Holy Spirit without a mental realization of what was taking place, and his words became as barbed arrows to strike conviction in those with whom he spoke, even on the streets.

Several years ago a ship sank in the Hudson River and greatly hindered the heavy traffic from the sea into the docks of the city. Removing this sunk ship proved to be a difficult task. Finally, one of the ordinary workmen made a brilliant suggestion. He assembled several barges and at low tide fastened the barges to the sunk vessel on the bottom of the Hudson. When the tide came in, the vessel was lifted. The workman's plan succeeded because it harnessed the mighty power of the Atlantic Ocean.[8] No soul is too hopeless and no case is too difficult for the mighty power of God.

Chapter 3

The Equipment
of the Soul-Winner

Every profession has its peculiar equipment. The artist has his brushes, palette, oils, and canvas. He must have above this physical equipment an inspiration. The farmer must have a great variety of plows, wagons, animals, and tractors, and a knowledge of the nature of his particular type of soil. In addition to this, he will read the best farm magazines and stay abreast with the very latest developments in agriculture. The lawyer, doctor, and soldier must have the equipment of their respective professions. The winner of souls must possess the necessary equipment.

Earnestness is an equipment of the soul-winner. The soul-winner must be sincere. If he is not in earnest, he cannot lead the lost to be so. If he is in earnest, it will be demonstrated in his anxiety for souls. It will come out in his conversation and in the tone of his voice. It will be witnessed in his tender persistence. It will manifest itself in his boldness and patience. Suppose he visits the sinner with the attitude, "Oh, well, you are lost, and I am a Christian; it is my duty to talk to you. The church has sent me to see if you would be interested in becoming a Christian; so here I am." No, he is not interested.

24

The sinner has very little knowledge, if any, about what it means to be a Christian. He may be enjoying sin, for the time at least. The soul-winner must be eager and positive. He must know that he has something to offer the lost that the lost cannot afford to be without.

He will announce the good news joyously and with life. The sports announcer describes a football game over the radio. The game is ordinary until a player catches a pass on his own thirty-five yard line and dashes through the arms of the opposition for a spectacular touchdown. How does the announcer describe the sixty-nine-yard run? Does he talk in a low, lackadaisical fashion, or do his voice and words flash with the animation and color of the moment? One's earnestness and pure enthusiasm will make oceans of difference to the person being approached.

Earnestness is born in tears. "He that goeth forth and weepeth, bearing precious seed, shall doubtless come again with rejoicing, bringing his sheaves with him" (Psalm 126:6). In this statement there are two requisites to bringing back the sheaves. They are concern born of tears and the precious seed of truth. Both are essential equipment of the witness. Our Lord wept over sinners, and you must weep over them if you are to win them.

Every time the writer has become heartbroken over sinners he has seen them respond freely. When a church prays and agonizes over lost souls, it reaps a golden harvest. People will give heed to anyone who displays a real concern for them. They may not follow, but they will give ear. For the soul-winner, this is an advantage for which he longs. Let the personal evangelist ask himself, "Who and what affected me most when I was lost?" He will remember that it was not brilliant sermons or speeches of talented orators. It was soulful earnestness. It was the person or the approach that revealed personal concern. The tears of an elderly Methodist woman did more for the writer before he was converted than all the sermons put together. This woman talked to me about my soul as she spoke to me in tears. I could not help but know that she was deeply interested in me.

This past summer the writer stood by the magnificent tomb of Napoleon in the Invalides in Paris by the Seine. I was moved as I recalled the mighty influence of "the little general." The effects of his cannon balls are seen as far away as the face of the Sphinx in Egypt. Without modern transportation facilities he took an army over the Alps. He was a man of ingenuity and indomitable courage, but his mightiest strength was in his earnestness and enthusiasm. His earnestness completely captivated his soldiers, and they in turn became almost invincible. His burning presence animated them with dauntless courage. When the soul-winner is animated by the earnestness of his Master, his actions will arrest the lost so that they cannot but choose to listen.

A Knowledge of the Bible Valuable

Recently a man came to the home of Finley Graham in Beirut, Lebanon, to talk to him about membership in the church. Fifteen years before that, when the man had been a customs officer on the Iraq border, someone had given him a New Testament. He read it and studied it, and now he and his family have accepted Christ as Saviour and are asking for church membership.

A few years ago a wild and irresponsible young man visited in the home of a certain pastor. While there, he began to read the individual Gospels which lay on the table in the living room of the pastor. When he left, he carried a pocket full of the little Gospels with him. The next time the pastor heard from him he had been converted, and today that young man is pastor of one of the most consistently evangelistic churches in Texas.

The Word of God is a fire and a hammer (Jer. 23:29). The Bible is vital, because it has effect on the witness as well as the sinner. All great soul-winners have been mighty in the Scriptures. There has never been an exception.

The Scriptures have a very definite effect on the soul-winner. One's attitude toward the Bible and his use of it will determine his effectiveness as a soul-winner.

A knowledge and use of the Word of God develops one spiritually.[1] God admonishes us to grow in grace (2 Peter 3:18). He explains just how this growth is possible. "As newborn babes, desire the sincere milk of the word, that ye may grow thereby" (1 Peter 2:2). The Word of God provides the strength of life. Men do not live by bread only, but by the Word of God (Matt. 4:4). The Word of God is to the spiritual man what bread is to the physical man. How much of the Bible could a soul-winner reproduce on paper if all the Bibles were burned? That is how much Bible he really knows.

A knowledge of the Bible gives the personal worker poise. He has confidence as he faces Satan in battle for a soul (Psalm 119:11). Our Lord quoted the Bible in answer to the temptations of Satan in the wilderness. Jesus repeatedly replied, "It is written" (Matt. 4:7). The psalmist found shelter and confidence in the Word: "So shall I have wherewith to answer him that reproacheth me: for I trust in thy word" (Psalm 119:42). Many are too timid to do personal evangelism because they are aware of their ignorance of the Bible. A thorough knowledge of the Word will replace such cowardice with courage.

The movie stars of Hollywood often memorize an entire book in order to play their parts in the picture and to get their fictitious message over the footlights. Medical doctors master multisyllabic words and memorize formulas in order to save life. We have a message of eternal truth, and we are physicians of the soul. Can we afford to give less energy and time to a study of our material, which is designed to save eternal souls?

A knowledge of the Bible makes for the effectiveness of the soul-winner. Dr. Charles Trumbull gives us an illustration which demonstrates the necessity of a thorough knowledge of

the Word of God if one is to win all types of lost men.[2] A young
rationalist was attracted to a revival meeting because of the
tremendous crowds which were in attendance. He was im-
pressed by the sincerity of the minister. He continued to attend
the services because of these two facts. He thought that Christianity was nothing more than an ingenious mythology with a
slender thread of historical truth in it.

Night after night he attended the revival and finally decided
to read the New Testament. When he had finished reading the
New Testament, he retired one night after the service to the
inquiry room. A consecrated soul-winner undertook to deal
with him.

The young rationalist said to the soul-winner: "Your Bible
teaches three things. It teaches first that Jesus is the Son of
God. Second, it teaches that salvation does not depend upon
our own righteousness but upon the death of Christ. Third, it
teaches the resurrection of Christ. Is that right?" The soul-
winner replied, "That is correct." The young man answered:
"I do not believe any one of these three fundamental preachments of the New Testament. I can't believe that Christ is the
Son of God. I do not believe that anyone can rise from the dead,
and I can't see how the death of one person could possibly
help anyone else."

The soul-winner took up his first objection. He questioned
the young man, "You say you are a rationalist; is that correct?"
The young man replied, "Yes, that is correct." "You are therefore a theist?" "Yes, I am a theist." Then said the soul-winner:
"You believe there is a God, and if you believe there is a God
and that God created the world, then you cannot deny the
philosophical possibility of God's coming down into his creation in any form that he may desire. He may come as a tree or
he may come as a bird or he may come as a human being."
"Yes, I can see that is possible, but it is not probable."

Then the young man added: "You see, Christ was deceived.
He said, 'I and my Father are one' (John 10:30). Then he

said, 'For my Father is greater than I' (John 14:28). Jesus also said, 'All power is given unto me' (Matt. 28:18). In one breath he says that he and his Father are one, and in another breath he admits that his Father is greater than he is; and then he goes on to say that his power is given to him of someone else and, if he receives his power from someone else, that someone is greater than he. Therefore, Jesus is contradicting himself."

The soul-winner moved very cautiously here, but his knowledge of the Bible greatly helped him. He simply pointed out to the young man that if he had been on earth and had heard Christ say these seemingly contradictory things and had gone to him for conference, Christ would have said, "My child, if for the purpose of your redemption from sin and from the curse of the law I voluntarily laid aside my eternal glory and limited my being to the condition of your nature that I might in that nature offer up to God such a sacrifice to enable God to forgive all who accept it, and then, after having made the atonement, I should give up my inferior position and return to my original glory, would there be anything wrong with that?" The soul-winner talked thus to the young man. He said: "Sure, that sounds fine. That would be wonderful if such had ever happened, but the Bible does not say anything like that anywhere."

Then the soul-winner turned hurriedly to Philippians 2 and read verses 5 through 8.

The young man took the Bible in his own hands with great astonishment and read the passage over again and again. Finally he said, "Wonderful! Wonderful!" and continued to hold the book in his hand; and with quivering lips he read part of the statement again and looked up into the face of the soul-winner and asked, "What have I got to do about it?"

The soul-winner quoted Romans 10:10 and urged him to accept Christ as Saviour and confess him.

The young man looked at him again and said, "I do believe in my heart that God raised him from the dead; and I do acknowledge him as my Saviour."

A thorough knowledge of the Word of God enabled this alert soul-winner to choose the exact passage of Scripture that was necessary to shed light upon the trouble of the young man and lead to his salvation.

The Bible has its effects on the sinner. It creates faith. "Faith cometh by hearing, and hearing by the word of God" (Rom. 10:17).

The Word of God is used to bring conviction to the sinner. "Now when they heard this, they were pricked in their heart, and said unto Peter and to the rest of the apostles, Men and brethren, what shall we do?" (Acts 2:37). The Word of God burns like a fire in the conscience and breaks the stony heart to pieces. "Is not my word like as a fire? saith the Lord; and like a hammer that breaketh the rock in pieces?" (Jer. 23:29).

The Word of God is used to work life in the individual. "Being born again, not of corruptible seed, but of incorruptible, by the word of God, which liveth and abideth for ever" (1 Peter 1:23).

The Message of the Soul-Winner

The source of the message is God. There is nothing in redeemed man that could give rise to the message of salvation. It is true that he has been converted, but the seed of his salvation did not originate within him. It was planted from without. The source of the redemptive message is the heart of God. It came out of the love of God (John 3:16). How God could love a rebellious, corrupt, evil-minded, lost soul is beyond our comprehension. Man loves the lovable and especially those who admire and appreciate him, but God loves the wicked and the hateful wretch. He loves those who hate him and who fight against him. He loves those who crucified his Son and would blot out his name (Luke 23:34).

The evangel came from the mercy of God. The sinner does not deserve mercy. He deserves damnation. The source of the redemptive evangel is not the nature of the sinner. Unredeemed man is hopeless; he lives under a heartless tyranny, and his needs are great. But being a sinner by choice as well as by nature renders him without deserts. There may be much room for polemics here, but there is no argument that his needs do not constitute the source of the gospel message. Out of the tender mercy of God came the design for redemption. God's mercy does not compel him to overlook the sins of men, but rather to provide a way of escape. Mercy is not the opposite of justice. Justice is the opposite of injustice. Mercy and justice are parts of the same. There is no justice apart from mercy, and no mercy apart from justice. The way of escape from sin must be in keeping with justice. The cross, therefore, is part of the message of redemption, because it reconciles justice and mercy.

It came from the determining mind of God. Some think that the message is too narrow and too personal to affect the world and history. It is narrow. It is so narrow that it confines success-ful and eternal living to only one way and one Saviour (Acts 4:12). It rules out all forms of paganism. It declares, "Come unto me, all ye that labour and are heavy laden, and I will give you rest" (Matt. 11:28). Did this narrow preachment affect the world? It has freed thousands of slaves and improved prison conditions. It has been the determining influence which has prevented child labor and made possible a living wage for laborers. Wherever it has been given a chance, it has made for better moral conditions. It has saved nations from bitter and bloody revolution. W. H. Lecky held that the Wesleyan revival in England saved the nation from the kind of bloodshed that throttled France, her neighbor.

The message is personal. The original gospel message was a testimony, a message suited for person-to-person delivery. It is primarily a dealing of person with person. This does not make it small; it makes it thorough and permanent. Since there are more than two billion people in the world, is it not a waste of energy to deal with one person? God ordained that the gospel would spread from heart to heart and not from mass to mass.

It is most effective. Dr. Gray used to say: "If there is placed before you a number of empty bottles and you throw a pail of water at the open bottles, some water will get into some of the bottles. If one wishes to fill all the bottles, let him take them one by one by the neck and place the pail to the mouth of the bottle and fill one at a time."

Giving a message person to person is not so slow as one may think. If a Christian wins one person to Christ each day, and each one he wins should win one each day, it would amount to 746,586,112 within one month. Within thirty-two days they would win more than 2,700,000,000. If each person won should win only one person a year, we could win the world in fifteen years. Of course, this is fantastic, but it should serve to open one's eyes to the possibility of the personal approach. We feel that each convert could win others, and would if led to. He should be urged to do it now as he learns. Through the method and message given by Christ our generation could win the world in less than a decade.

Adam sinned against God and fell from his lofty place before God. As a result, all mankind went astray. God determined to bring men back. They were free agents, and he could not coerce them. He therefore sent his Son to earth to call men back to him. The plan was conceived in the mind of God.

The spirit of the message was manifest in the ministry of Christ. When publicans and sinners drew near to him to hear him, the religionists murmured because Christ received sinners and associated with them. He justified his actions by asking them, "What man of you, having an hundred sheep, if he lose one of them, doth not leave the ninety and nine in the wilderness, and go after that which is lost, until he find it?" (Luke 15:4). Then he added, "Likewise joy shall be in heaven over one sinner that repenteth, more than over ninety and nine just persons, which need no repentance" (Luke 15:7). The evangelist must catch the spirit of his message.

The spirit is joyous. The soul-winner loses all sense of duty in the joy of his proclamation. He would cross the ocean to preach one message. He would endure almost any kind of hardship to witness for his Master.

The spirit of the message is humility. The messenger will never discriminate between men. He will preach to all mankind, irrespective of race or color. One's station in society will make no difference. Just as Christ ministered to the publicans and sinners, the Phenicians and the Samaritans, so will the soul-winner minister to all peoples.

The spirit of the message is uncompromising. The witness will never apologize for his message. He believes in his evangel. He believes that it is distinctive; he believes that it contains the hope of the world; he regards a declaration of it as the highest privilege on earth. He will stand like the son of a king and proclaim it. He will not trim the message to suit the trends of the times. When the message is trimmed, it bleeds to death. The evangel should never be disguised in order to get it past an unbeliever's guard.[3] The spirit of the message requires that it be presented in bold outline and free from all camouflage.

Certain aspects characterize the gospel message.

It is Christ centered. Christ is the subject of the gospel. There is no evangel without Christ. The message is about him. It is not a moral message. One may preach on moral ills and remedies if he chooses, but let him remember that he is not necessarily preaching the gospel. The righteousness of Christ is not moral living. Moral living is one of the fruits of the righteousness of Christ, but men do not live socially and morally correct in order to be saved. Moral ills will be remedied only as people receive a changed nature. Any sermon in the New Testament will give full proof that the gospel message is about Christ.

The soul-winner does not need to answer all related questions in the message to a lost man. Men are tempted to convert the mighty facts in the life of Christ into problems.[4] Soul-winners often lose themselves and their chance to win the lost by trying to argue questions like the virgin birth and related doctrines. Things which may pose difficulty for theologians have never entered the minds of lost men, and it is thus not necessary to air those things or find a solution before the sinner can be led to accept Christ. When the soul-winner finds a lost man who is confused about some doctrinal difficulty, if he will tell him that it is not required that he understand that particular problem in order to be saved, it will greatly help. When questions are raised, it is better to tell the person that we shall take that question up later, but his relation to God must be settled first. The result will usually be a joyous one. The sinner will put aside that problem and accept Christ. Dr. Mullins says, "Direct the mind and heart of the inquirer away from all other problems; direct it toward a personal trust in the once crucified but now living Christ." [5]

The message will be stated simply. Non-Christians are often confused by our theological terms. It is essential that we speak their language. In two minutes of conversation the soul-winner will realize the extent of the education of the prospect and will make the message plain. The soul-winner must be familiar with the process of salvation. It is not necessary that the lost person understand the process. The relation of the personal witness and the sinner is the same as that of the doctor and patient. The patient need not understand the ingredients of the prescription and how it affects him, but the doctor must. The witness knows that the new birth is the process, but he need not try to explain it. He may simply state that it is necessary to be transformed by the Word of God.

He knows that men are not made Christians by goodness, but because of their relation to God. One becomes a child of God by birth into God's family (John 3:7). General William Booth said, "The world's immediate and greatest peril is that the church will offer the world a philosophy of Christianity that provides forgiveness without regeneration." [6] God originally made man in his image; sin defaced that image. The image must be restored; it is restored through the new birth (Titus 3:5). God made us. It becomes necessary that he remake us. It is impossible to teach the unregenerate man to be a child of God. He must be taught the need of salvation and led to follow Christ, but God must change him. It is the work of God to change man's sinful nature. When men are led to yield to God, God gladly regenerates them.

The soul-winner will hasten to show that the new relation to God is made possible because of what Christ has done. It is based on the meritorious work of Christ on the cross.

It is a saving message. It declares man's spiritual need. All are under the penalty of death: "All have sinned" (Rom. 3:23). "All" takes in everyone. By sin "all we like sheep have gone astray" (Isa. 53:6). To be astray is to be away from God, and to be away from God is to be lost. "The wages of sin is death" (Rom. 6:23). If all have sinned, then all are under the penalty of death. If the sinner is standing chained by sin in the path of death, he is in great need. Very few sinners will be audacious enough to argue their innocence. Some may disclaim their sins. The message will point up that the greatest sin is the rejection of Christ. The fact that they have not accepted Christ as Saviour makes them guilty of unbelief (John 3:18). Because of unbelief they are under the wrath of God: "He that believeth not the Son shall not see life; but the wrath of God abideth on him" (John 3:36).

The lost are doomed. Isaiah showed his generation how it was doomed by separation from God: "Your iniquities have separated between you and your God, and your sins have hid his face from you, that he will not hear" (Isa. 59:2). Their sins of murder, bodily iniquity, and lying lips had driven a wedge between them and God. Their shame had drawn a thick curtain which obscured God's face. Sin had so separated that God could not hear their prayers. Separation from God is the worst effect of sin. Nothing is so distressing and painful as separation from God, the source of life.

When Jesus bore our sin in his body on the tree, it was necessary for God to turn his face away temporarily. God could not look upon sin with any degree of pleasure. When he looked away, it had a terrible effect. Christ was the Son of God and knew why he had been separated from the Father. He knew that God would turn again his face to him. Yet, it was such hell that Jesus cried out that bloodcurdling cry, "My God, my God, why hast thou forsaken me?" If temporary separation from God is that awful, how sore must it be to be eternally separated from God!

All need a Saviour. No man can save himself. The sinner is "dead in trespasses and sins" (Eph. 2:1). A dead man cannot walk or speak; he has no life in him. He lies chained in helplessness. To add to his incompetency to save himself, he is by nature a child of wrath (Eph. 2:3). He has no goodness of his own; the savior must come from without. The Saviour is Christ: "Being justified freely by his grace through the redemption that is in Christ Jesus" (Rom. 3:24). "Therefore we conclude that a man is justified by faith without the deeds of the law" (Rom. 3:28). The Bible further declares that "neither is there salvation in any other: for there is none other name under heaven given among men, whereby we must be saved" (Acts 4:12). Notice that here the verb for "saved" is an imperative which rules out completely the possibility that salvation could ever come from any other source or person.

The message sets forth God's provision for lost men. The motive of the message is the love of God (John 3:16). The love of God for sordid man will remain a mystery for all eternity. We possibly shall never fathom the meaning of his pure love for his wayward creatures. He did not look with pity on sinners; he deeply loved them. Out of this love grew God's provision for the redemption of fallen man.

He provided salvation through grace (Eph. 2:8). Grace is honor and favor. It is that absolute necessity which only God can provide. Man not only did not earn salvation, but he could not. Grace embraces forgiveness: "And you, being dead in your sins . . . hath he quickened together with him, having forgiven you all trespasses" (Col. 2:13). Removal of guilt depends upon forgiveness. Forgiveness is essential to fellowship between God and man. The offense must be buried beneath the blood, and tides of confidence and mutual good will must flow so high as to bury forever from view the cause of alienation. When this transpires, forgiveness is in effect and one is reconciled to God.

Grace is based upon the work of the cross. In the cross, the offender is not seeking reconciliation. The offended makes overtures to the offender. God has been sinned against by rebellious man; man is the offender. Through the cross God opens a way for offending man to return to fellowship with him. The cross stands as an eternal and impressive invitation to the prodigal to come back to God. It is more than an invitation; it is an open door. It is the old account settled in full and signed in God's blood. "The preaching of the cross is to them that perish foolishness; but unto us which are saved it is the power of God" (1 Cor. 1:18). The message of the soul-winner reveals how one may receive salvation. While God provides and offers salvation, man is accountable for receiving or rejecting it. It is generally accepted that man must repent and believe. Man cannot repent and believe on his own initiative. God works these graces in man, but man must co-operate.

Repentance is required (Luke 13:3). Repentance is a change which affects the whole man. It is a change of the mind, and it also extends into the emotions. "For godly sorrow worketh repentance to salvation" (2 Cor. 7:10). It embraces a change of disposition toward God and a change of attitude toward sin. Through repentance one takes a position before God. He turns to God from his sins as he is assisted by applied truth. The Holy Spirit uses truth to work godly sorrow and a determination to desert evil. The sinner must repent when God works repentance in him. He cannot choose the time or place when he will repent; he must move under direct compulsion. Isaiah pleaded with his people when God was moving among them, "Seek ye the Lord while he may be found, call ye upon him while he is near" (Isa. 55:6).

Faith is essential. Living faith is in a person (John 3:16). It is not faith in a creed or a system. In every place in the New Testament where saving faith is referred to, it is in connection with a person and not a system (John 3:18, 36; Acts 16:30–31; etc.). Believing is receiving. "As many as received him, to them gave he power to become the sons of God, even to them that believe on his name" (John 1:12). One becomes a son of God through the power of God. He receives this power by receiving Christ, and he receives Christ by believing.

Prayer an Essential Part

When a moment of opportunity approaches and a certain person arises to meet the occasion and wins a great victory, his world generally thinks only of the tactics he used and the brilliant thinking he displayed at the time. People would designate him a genius, but he and his teachers know that back of that personal achievement are long hours of study and energy put into preparation. He remembers the severe discipline and careful planning for such an event. He was made ready for the occasion by hard work.

In soul-winning, we are workers together with Him. One's spirit and attitude must be correct. This is where prayer serves as the most effective equipment of the individual evangelist. Through prayer come direction and power. Daily spiritual intercourse with God is necessary if the soul-winner would have the reinforcement required in rising to meet difficult challenges. To live without prayer is to be powerless.

A quiet time with God every day will prepare one to accomplish more for God. Luther said: "If I fail to pray two hours every morning, the devil gets the victory through the day. I have so much business that I cannot get on without spending three hours daily in prayer." Joseph Alleine arose at 4:00 A.M. and prayed until eight. He called early prayer his business. If he heard laborers up working before he got up, he would say in embarrassment: "Oh, how this shames me! Does not my Master deserve more than theirs?" John Welch, the wonderful Scotch preacher, thought his day ill spent if he did not spend eight hours in prayer.

A quiet time set aside each day for prayer will make the message sharp. It will enable God to come down into the message of the soul-winner. Prayer is a ladder by which God comes down into the heart and into the sermon. God thus is moved toward the people, and God must be moved toward the people before the people can be moved toward God. Prayer is, therefore, basic in the life of the soul-winner. No soul-winner should venture to plead with men until he has first pleaded with God.

Prayer is the most serious obligation of the soul-winner. So much depends on prayer that it becomes more than an individual privilege. It becomes a binding obligation. The medical doctor is obligated to use his skill to help the suffering and to save life. Likewise, the witness is impelled to pray for the lost. He is propelled by the clear record of the Bible and history.

The prayers of Moses marked the turning point in the history of his nation. His people had lapsed into idolatry. The judgment of God was upon them. Moses' prayers stayed the judgment of God and made way for a mighty spiritual refreshing that changed the entire course of the people. Hezekiah's prayers turned back from the gates the threat of national oblivion. Out of the prayers of Samuel at Mizpah came a spiritual upsurgence that spelled the birth of a nation.

Mrs. Sarah Wesley prayed one hour every day. She had nineteen children; she was the wife of a pastor; she had many church duties besides caring for nineteen children; yet she shut herself in a closet with God one hour every day. It is no wonder that she reared a son named Charles who wrote more than six thousand hymns and whose golden throat sang down from heaven to earth the very angels of glory. No wonder she reared a son named John who took two continents by the heartstrings and brought them to the feet of God.

No real witness will want to escape the obligation of prayer. No conscientious witness would care to go to the judgment with blood on his hands caused by prayerlessness. No true-hearted believer would miss the joy of seeing thousands set free through a ministry made effective by prayer.

Prayer enables the witness to use the Bible effectively. Through prayer a person becomes acutely aware of the presence of God. One need not attempt to make God present; he can know God is there. By prayer he reaches out and feels God. If one is conscious of the living presence of God as he reads the Bible, its truths will come alive. We shall behold it as the revelation of God, in whose presence we read.[7]

Chapter 4

The Approach

The approach is the first step in the operation of soul-winning. The approach may determine the conclusion. Every mountain peak, regardless of how precipitous, has at least one avenue of access. The experienced mountain climber will climb cautiously and watch for any sign of an accessible approach. He will find it. Every experienced soul-winner will listen carefully to his prospect and study his peculiarities and bent of mind until he locates the avenue to his soul. There is no man who cannot be effectively approached for Christ. There is an entrance or contact point somewhere. The successful soul-winner will work patiently until he has found that approach.[1] The approach is as essential to the decision as it is to the instructions.

The approach is tuning in on your man. The light waves may be filled with an attractive television program, but the program will not be seen unless it is tuned in on the television set. To make a proper approach is to capture the attention, but it is more than that.

The approach is stimulating a real interest. The approach is to the soul-winner what the punch line is to the salesman. The approach must whet a desire to see what comes next. It must make one want the product being offered.

The approach is to the successful witness what the lure is to

41

the fisherman. The fisherman must have bait, and no fisherman would use the same lure every time he fishes. The situation, the type of fish, and the waters in which one is fishing will determine the bait. The skill with which he uses the lure enhances the prospects of success. The approach is the starting point. It is the way to begin. To catch a fish, one must first begin. The fisherman begins when he casts his lure into the waters. The fisherman does not walk up to the stream and splash the water and yell, "Look at me! I'm here," and then gracefully throw out the lure. Rather, he avoids drawing attention to himself, for he may frighten the fish away.

The successful soul-winner will hide behind the cross and, without attracting attention to himself, practice the art of catching men for Christ. Whether the approach is classified direct or indirect, let it originate at the cross.

The Determining Factors

The situation is a determining factor. Three things enter the situation: the person, the place, and the time.

The background and condition of the prospect will alter the approach. The sex, profession, and age will be carefully considered. The farmer and the lawyer live vastly different lives and have different problems. Two men in the same profession will be poles apart in disposition, attitude, and background; but all, regardless of profession, have one thing in common—they are sinners. They need a Saviour. For this reason, a knowledge of general principles will serve a great purpose. No soul-winner will slavishly stick to any studied rule. He will remain alert and will vary the approach as well as the instructions. It is often essential to meet the problems of men and answer the fundamental questions which hinder them, but to do this is not necessarily to win the prospect to Christ. It often requires more time for the truth to become a part of the person than some soul-winners think. Some may grasp it immediately, while others may not.

The place is a definite part of the situation.

If a person is sick and is in the hospital, this fact will color the contact. If he is severely sick and death is near, one would go immediately into the need for Christ as Saviour and tell him how to embrace Christ as Saviour and how to do so now.

If the person is normal and the approach is made in the home, the beginning would be more casual but no less determined. The home is an excellent place for soul-winning, if there are no abnormal distractions, if the rest of the family sit quietly and talk only when asked to respond.

If the wife is prone to nag her husband to become a Christian, it is never wise to approach him in her presence. Take him away in your car and talk to him in private. When dealing with a family, always talk to the one most interested first. Win him, then turn to the others one at a time.

The contact may be made in the church. There are three excellent occasions to win souls in a church service: before the service begins, during the invitation song, and after the service has been dismissed. At the close of the service is one of the very best times. The person's interest has been heightened by the service, and he is still under the power of the gospel. Speak kindly, sympathetically, and lovingly to him after you have taken him to one side and away from the hearing of the others. The writer has often seen people under conviction in a revival service and after the service taken them aside and won them to Christ before they left the building.

People of your own sex may be approached on the streets or in public places like depots or trains. Unless one is very wise, seasoned, and has real love for the lost, he should be very cautious in this situation. One may do more harm than good unless he is directed by the Holy Spirit.

The time enters very definitely into the situation. The time is less important than the other elements, but often it is a determining element. The amount of knowledge of the Scriptures, the purpose of the church, and the plan of salvation is vital. If the prospect has no knowledge of spiritual matters, it will require more time to make the approach. There must be a good foundation for a decision.

It is also important to bear in mind that if the person being dealt with is in a hurry to make an appointment, the soul-winner will wait for another occasion. Often the religious visitor will enter a home and find a family engaged in looking at a favorite television program. In this case, he will be wise to excuse himself and tell them that he will return later and, if possible, make a date to return when they will not be engaged in something which is of interest to them. The time element is vital in soul-winning.

The leading of the Holy Spirit is the greatest factor in the approach. When one is sensitive to the presence of the Holy Spirit, he will recognize his leadings. He will not confuse personal ambitions and fleshly desires with the plain, pure leadings of the Spirit. The soul-winner must never substitute anything for the leadings of the Spirit. A program of activity is fine so long as it does not interfere with the Spirit or even supplant his leadings.

Ananias was led by the Holy Spirit to go to a certain home on the street called Straight in Damascus and speak to one called Saul (Acts 9:11). His approach was direct and effective. Ananias had never seen Saul before, as far as we know, but he had heard of the havoc which Saul had wrought on the church. When convinced that God was leading him, he made the approach. Saul responded and was baptized. The Holy Spirit was working at both ends of the line. He had convicted Saul before he led Ananias to talk to him. The soul-winner can be sure that God does everything well. He works at both ends of the line and will have the heart ready for his coming.

The attitude of the soul-winner is an important factor. The superior attitude is a hindrance to the soul-winner. Steer clear of the holier-than-thou attitude.[2] If one is sincere, he will be free from this hindrance. The sincere person rarely causes resentment. Paul warns us not to think more highly of ourselves than we ought (Rom. 12:3). God instructs his workers, "Gird yourselves with humility, to serve one another" (1 Peter 5:5, ASV). The evangelist must fling his demolishing missiles from an humble heart. If one is not able to talk about revealed truth in the spirit of true humility, it is evident that the truth is not real to him. The superior attitude is not conducive to preaching the cross. That which is basic in redeeming truth will be omitted or hidden by the holier-than-thou complex.

The soul-winner must be as free from the inferior attitude as he is from the superior attitude. He is not to quail before men. The apostle Paul was free from the superiority complex, yet he was very bold and even forward at times (Acts 13:10-11). God cannot use the proud; but then, neither can he use the coward.

To be humble does not make one less a man. John said, "He that cometh after me is mightier than I, whose shoes I am not worthy to bear" (Matt. 3:11). John was humble, but he was not fearful. The same John spoke in disarming boldness to the multitudes from Jerusalem, Judea, and the regions around Jordan, saying, "O generation of vipers, who hath warned you to flee from the wrath to come?" (Matt. 3:7). Do not be afraid to try to win others; thousands of souls go lost every year into eternity because redeemed people are afraid to try.

John Mark went out upon the ministry of Christ and took along a lunch for one boy, and that lunch fed five thousand. He was willing to give unto Christ what was in his hands, and Christ multiplied it and blessed it to the physical strengthening of five thousand people (John 6:4-11). Some may have more talents than others, but those with less talents are to use what God has given unto them.

The writer was conducting a revival campaign in an oil city, and at the close of one of the morning services a man past sixty years of age came forward on profession of faith. When the people had dispersed, he said to me, "Do you know why I came forward this morning asking for church membership as a candidate for baptism?"

I said, "No, sir, but I would certainly like to know."

Then the elderly gentleman told me that a few weeks before he had been sick, and some little Junior boys had come to see him and brought a basket of fruit. When they started to leave, they asked him if they might have a word of prayer. He said he felt ashamed not to permit them to pray for him. He said the little boys knelt by his bed and prayed for him. When they left, he said to himself: "You rascal, you! Here you are with one foot in the grave and the other on the brink of the grave, and these little boys have more interest in your salvation than you do."

He said that his conscience became so smitten after the little boys left that he got down on his knees right where they had knelt and gave his heart to Christ. He continued, "That is why I came this morning."

These little boys did not know very much about soul-winning, but they used what knowledge they had. They did not know what to say to the elderly man, but they prayed for him in his presence, and God used it. We must be willing to use what God has placed in our hands.

There are several reasons why people are too timid to approach lost men.

Many are timid because they are overconcerned with themselves. They fear that they will fail. They realize that they have had no experience in winning the lost, and they do not know enough to start. Because of this, they back away. The inferiority complex grows out of an abnormal concern for self, and may be cured by an enlarged concern for others. The glaring needs of others often help one to forget his limitations. This lack of confidence can also be removed by a solid effort to help others.

A fine Christian woman who longed to see her husband come to Christ was too timid to speak to him about the matter. She was enlisted by the pastor to win others. She was placed on the team with an experienced soul-winner. In the first home they entered, two people trusted Christ. In the next home one accepted Christ. When they left that home, the timorous woman excused herself and went straight home. She had seen God save three people that night. It had convinced her that she could win her husband. When she arrived at home, she went immediately to his room and, with enlarged concern and confidence, won him with amazing ease.

Others are timorous because of the wrong conception of soul-winning. They have been led to think that it requires great knowledge and skill in argument. They feel that by force of logic one imposes his ideas on another. Being leery of this technique, they shy away from soul-winning. They must be told that the soul-winner avoids polemics and would never use coercion. They are to be told also that many hungry hearts are longing to be contacted and would gladly welcome an approach.

A soul-winner once approached a famous businessman with a degree of nervousness. However, he asked the man with an air of apology if he were a Christian. The great businessman seized the hand of the soul-winner with great emotion and urged, "Do not ever hesitate to speak to any man about his soul!" and then went on to say that he had longed for twenty years for some Christian to speak to him. He expressed the opinion that there were thousands of people in the same condition who are not courageous enough to ask for help, but would willingly accept it.[3] If the timid Christian can be led to realize this, it will serve to bolster his courage and provide the necessary impetus.

The attitude of the Christian can be greatly strengthened if he realizes that he is not doing a strange thing but a normal thing when he seeks to win others to Christ. If a soul-winner feels that he is doing an unnatural thing when he contacts the lost, it will weaken his approach. One must realize that sinners are abnormal. Sin curbs life and bewilders the victim. The soul-winner is seeking to restore normalcy. Thus, we conclude that evangelism is an effort to make normal persons out of abnormal ones.[4]

Some False Approaches

One of these is the traditional method. It is seldom ever wise to begin by asking the individual, "Are you a Christian?" Many a person thinks he is a Christian and in all honesty will answer in the affirmative. In many quarters people are so confused and so poorly informed about what it means to be a Christian that they believe that all human beings are, in a sense, Christians. This idea is predominant in any country or locality where the Catholics are strong. Some think that because they were christened when a baby, this act made them Christians. Some also take church membership for salvation. Much religious teaching in the world is shallow, superficial, and unscriptural. As a result of this, it is seldom wise to begin the approach with the question, "Are you a Christian?"

Chester Wilkins, Jr., went from house to house with his Bible in his hand. The folks saw his Bible and turned him away because it was a Catholic community. He asked God for guidance. He then concealed his Bible and knocked on the door and began by saying: "I am here to talk about the most valuable thing in the world. It is so valuable that the richest man cannot buy it, and yet the poorest man can have all he wants. It will give you peace and contentment for today and hope for tomorrow. It will pay bigger dividends than anything in the world, and it will keep you when all else fails." He would sharpen their interest before letting them know just exactly what he was driving at. Once he had got their attention and entered the house, he would begin talking to them about salvation in Christ. And at the proper time he would take his little concealed New Testament from his pocket and begin to read it to them.[5]

It is well also to avoid asking the question, "Are you a sinner?" John was a great evangelist and disciple. He learned what he knew directly from Jesus. He caught his spirit from Christ also. It would be well to study his approach. Did he ever ask, "Do you know you are a sinner?" Of course he did not, because they did not know they were sinners. Sometimes men are conscious of the fact that they are sinners, but ordinarily no one is more blind to his sins than the sinner. He is dead in trespasses and sin. Dead men cannot see their blindness. Many sinners are satisfied with their secular living. They are pleased with themselves and with their world. They see no need of God in their lives. They have no sense of sin. They must be led to know that they are sinners; but merely asking the question will not reveal their sin to them.

Another traditional approach which must be avoided is to ask the question, "Are you a church member?" An experienced soul-winner once asked a stranger, "Have you been born twice?" The man replied, "No, I have been born only once." He invited the soul-winner into his home and told him that he was a church member but had never been born again. Before the soul-winner left the home, the man was saved. If the soul-winner had asked, "Are you a Christian?" he would have answered, "Yes," for he felt that his church relationship settled that.[6]

There are times when any of these traditional questions may be asked and properly used. If the soul-winner knows well the background of the person with whom he is dealing, then he may safely ask any one of these questions in order to begin the conversation. But if he is uncertain, then it is never safe to use these questions.

Do not spotlight the sinner nor the soul-winner. If the sinner is magnified in the approach, he may immediately go on the defense. There are cases when it is not necessary to point up one's sins in order to bring conviction. These cases, however, are generally exceptional, but it is necessary to be familiar with them. A recognition of one's position before God will not of itself work conviction. The Holy Spirit is the only one who can convict the sinner. Remember Christ is the subject of the gospel. Preach Christ, and touch on sin only as it prevents fellowship with Christ and what our sins cost Christ. This is the truth that the Holy Spirit uses to bring conviction. The sinner will never see the awfulness of his sins until he looks at them through Christ. To see Christ is to love him; to see Christ is to be drawn to him (John 12:32). When one is drawn to Christ, he is drawn away from sin. The purpose of sin is to separate from God. When God and man are reconciled through Christ, sin loses its power. Preach Christ primarily and sin incidentally, but in no case magnify the sinner. It is always well to begin where the issue centers—in Christ and his claims.

If the soul-winner spotlights himself, then he and his imperfections will loom up. The sinner will not be able to see Christ because of the overmagnified presence and personality of the soul-winner. The only time the soul-winner would speak of himself would be to show how Christ saved him and from what depths of sin the Lord was able to lift him. He will never magnify his troubles or anything else in particular connected with his life.

Do not condemn. An evangelist and a friend visited in a home recently to urge that the father and mother move their church membership and bring their little son into the Sunday school of the church. The pastor asked, "How long have you been living here?" She told him, "For ten months." He said, "You've been living here ten months and have not united with some church yet?"

She replied: "That is correct. We have been here but have not started to church yet."

The pastor then said: "There is something wrong with your brand of religion. Anybody who can move to a new place and live there that long and have a little child the age of your son and not attend church, there is something wrong with their religion."

This was plain talk, and it was true; but it was unwise to say it. It was not necessary to make those statements. To make such statements is only to offend and to drive the person away. The soul-winner must be dominated with a love in his heart for the lost and for the unchurched. He must not go out to drive them in. He must go out as a true shepherd to bring them in by leadership and by love.

Do not nag. The mother who nags her teen-age son about giving his heart to the Lord is sure to fail. Nagging always breeds resentment and disintegrates into boredom. No insurance salesman would think of annoying a prospect. If the prospect was not in the humor to talk about insurance, he would certainly not continue to talk with him. He would wait for a more convenient time. Sincere and well-placed words will get results, but a continual nagging never succeeds. The Sunday school teacher will be very cautious in dealing with that individual in her class who is unsaved. She will never let her interest and her concern bring her to the point of pestering or annoying the individual.

The Proper Approach

There are two types of approach. They are the indirect and the direct approach.

The indirect approach is more suitable to some people than the direct approach. Every soul-winner should use both approaches, but the approach which gets for him the greatest results is the one he will use most often. We generally think of the indirect approach as the cultivative approach.

The soul-winner will steer away from any type of fanaticism and will be very diplomatic. He will make contacts with the person he wishes to win. He will invite him to come to church with him. He will invite him out to lunch. He will take him places in his car. He will cultivate him. He will let the person know that he is vitally interested in him as an individual before he ever approaches him concerning his soul. It is often necessary to win the confidence of an individual before you can win him to Christ. If persons believe in you, then you can lead them to believe in Christ. If they think you are worth knowing, then it is easy to lead them to recognize that it is worth knowing Christ also and to know Christ as Saviour.

When the soul-winner feels that he has won the confidence of the individual and that the time is right to make the approach, then he will talk directly to him about Christ as Saviour. There are some people with whom this type of approach is most effective. In the indirect approach the soul-winner will always do that which he is not expected to do.

One Sunday afternoon recently a young pastor walked down the country road to his little church with his Bible under his arm. A stranger who lived in the community came along, saw him walking, and picked him up in his car. On the way to the church, in the course of the conversation, the stranger found out that the man was pastor of the church. When the man got out of the car, he thanked the stranger very kindly but did not invite him to stay for church and hear him preach.

This aroused interest on the part of the lost man because he did not expect the young pastor to make any such approach. He drove on up the road and then came back to the church-yard and parked and spoke with some of the church members about the young pastor. He told them that he had been surprised that the young man had not even invited him to hear him preach. Possibly out of curiosity more than anything else, he remained to hear the young preacher. The message was a gospel message. The stranger's heart was greatly warmed; he finally came back to accept Christ as Saviour.

If the young pastor had made an expected approach, it would have been so ordinary that he might not have made any impression at all upon the prospect. The pastor said later that he was keenly aware of what he was doing, that he did it on purpose. He added that he had been able to win many others by a similar approach.

The direct approach is possibly the most fruitful and most acceptable approach of all. We shall, therefore, discuss many direct approaches which we consider to be correct.

The best approach is to begin by telling the person about Christ. The soul-winner will not begin at all without knowing something about the individual. He will have a previous knowledge of his prospect, or he will talk with him long enough to be able to diagnose the situation; because the best approach is no approach at all until you have gathered certain vital information about the individual. The souls of men are too precious to use slipshod methods and tactless approaches. A great battle is to be won or lost. It is never wise to wage a decisive battle without planned strategy. If the soul-winner is convinced that the person to whom he is talking is not a Christian, then he should preach Christ to him and press the claims of Christ.

It would be the testimony of the greatest soul-winners that they have won to Christ many persons to whom they had never spoken before but very few of whom they knew nothing before the approach. John was a great soul-winner, and he always began by preaching Jesus. He would tell first who Jesus was (John 1:3). He told, in the second place, how Jesus came to give men power to become sons of God (John 1:11–12). In the next place, John instructed men how to be saved (John 1:12–13). John then ended the chapter by giving an illustration of how one receives this salvation through Christ (John 1:29, 35–51).[7] John gave much emphasis to the power of Christ to save.

Christ had divine power to heal the suffering. He did not exercise it on all occasions to validate his spiritual claim. He often saved men from sickness out of his deep compassion for the sufferer. Sometimes his miracles served as signs. The signs were evidences of his deity. John used several of these signs as proof of the divine power of Jesus. These great miracles often stimulated saving faith. It was for this express purpose that Jesus performed them before men, and it was for this reason that John and the other evangelists used them in the body of their Gospels. The most effective method employed, therefore, by the early evangelists was to preach Christ to lost men.

When men see their sins through the presence of Christ, and when they see the holiness of Jesus and the unselfish life and the death of Christ on the cross for their sins, it often does more to convict them than any other preachment which the soul-winner could use. There are many other points of contact and introductory ideas, but all of them must lead directly to the person of Christ.

Let the soul-winner begin with a point of interest. Dr. R. A. Hume, one of the most skilful soul-winners that ever served in Asia, was giving an account of how he won a Hindu in India to a saving knowledge of Christ. He said that one morning he came out of his house and saw a man leading a goat with a red band around its horns. He knew what it signified, but, in order to make an approach, he pretended not to know. He began by saying: "Good morning, my friend. Where are you going with that goat?"

"Oh, I'm going to the temple."

"May I go with you?"

"Why, do you want to go with me to the temple? Sure, you may go!"

Dr. Hume further inquired, "What are you going to do with that goat?"

The individual somewhat reluctantly said: "The goat is to be killed. I shall sacrifice it."

"Why do you kill the goat?" inquired Dr. Hume.

"I don't know."

"You don't know? Surely there must be some reason for it."

"If there is a reason, I do not know what it is."

Dr. Hume further questioned him, "But, there must be some reason."

"No, there is no reason as far as I know; it's just one of our customs." As he made that statement, he pointed back over his shoulder, "It came out of the past; it was done by our fathers."

Dr. Hume said again, "But you must have some reason for killing the goat."

"I don't know why."

Dr. Hume asked: "Is it because there is some sense of wrong, of sin, in your heart? And is it because you feel that something must die to satisfy it?"

"I just don't know, sir."

"Well, then, why do you have a red band around the horns of the goat? Why don't you have a white or a black band?"

Again the man answered: "I do not know. It is just one of our customs."

Dr. Hume insisted, "It must be for some reason."

Then Dr. Hume asked again, "Could it be that the red band symbolizes the color of the blood of the goat which is to be slain?"

"Oh, no," said the Indian. "I don't know; nobody does. It has existed for ages, and nobody really knows."

Then said Dr. Hume: "Excuse me; I know where it originated. And that is why I have come from America to live in India—to tell you and your people about it." The missionary began there and simply pointed out the story of the early sacrifices recorded in the Scriptures from Abel down to the days of Christ, and that Christ came as a fulfilment of this symbol and to pour out his blood a libation for the sins of men. He showed that the spilled blood of the goat was a symbol of the blood of the Saviour who would come to save them. And thus, beginning with something of religious interest to the Indian, the missionary effectively preached Christ to him.[8]

Often a man's child is of greater interest to him than anything else in the world. The Sunday school teacher has a great opportunity to win the lost men and women who have children in their respective classes. The writer has won many a man to Christ by taking an interest in the man's son and winning that son and making of him a dear friend; then later I would

visit the parents and talk to them about the fine boy and gain
entrance to their confidence by knowing personally many
things about their own son, possibly some things which they
did not know.

One may begin with the occupation of the individual. Every
person is vitally interested in his own profession; therefore,
the wise soul-winner would do well to familiarize himself with
the various professions so that he could talk intelligently about
any of them with the individuals.

The farmer.—You may begin with the farmer by telling him
that he is signally blessed by having a profession that is so close
to life and his closeness to life enables him readily to understand many of the great secrets of life. The soul-winner may
point out to him that he has a better foundation for appreciat-
ing Christ's teachings than men of almost any other profession.

Then use Christ's farm illustration about the grain of wheat:
"Except a corn of wheat fall into the ground and die, it
abideth alone: but if it die, it bringeth forth much fruit" (John
12:24). Jesus pointed up here that death is not what it appears
to be. Death is a seal of failure for unsaved men, but for Christians it is a condition of success.[9] Death for the Christian is not
the end, but the beginning. Death is the entrance into real life.
Paul said, "To die is gain." The passage from death to life was
brought to the knowledge of men by Christ.

Every farmer knows that a grain of corn must be planted in
the ground and die to produce life and multiply. From this
vantage point, the soul-winner can press home the great truth
of the new birth. Explain to the farmer that he may not be able
to understand the new birth, but he must accept it for himself
just as he accepts the truth about the corn of wheat, although
he does not understand that process. Show him that to die with
Christ does for him and his life just what the death of the
grain of wheat did for it. Show him that it is the beginning of a
more abundant life.

The doctor.—Great and busy men have tender hearts and

may be reached by honest and simple means. One does not have to be a scientist nor does he have to know too much about medical science in order to win a doctor or a scientist to Christ. A simple truth faithfully presented or a single passage of Scripture properly used may do the work.

A little girl was very sick. The doctor and nurses told the child on whom they were about to perform an operation, "Now we must put you to sleep before we can make you get better." The little girl replied, "I must say my prayers, for every night before I go to sleep I pray." Then she got off the bed and knelt and prayed: "Now, Lord, I lay me down to sleep; I pray thee, Lord, my soul to keep. If I should die before I wake, I pray thee, Lord, my soul to take." By the time she had finished praying, the doctor and nurses were wiping tears from their eyes. That doctor went home that night to kneel and pray for the first time in twenty years.

The carpenter.—It is comparatively easy to contact a carpenter. One may begin by discussing his honored profession. Tell him that the Saviour grew up in a carpenter shop in Nazareth. Show him that he used his knowledge of carpentry to illustrate a sermon on life (Matt. 7:24-27). One man built his house upon the sand, and it could not stand the stress and pressure of the storms; so it fell, and its ruin was complete. The other man was wise, for he selected a better foundation. He built his house upon the rock, and it stood the pressure of the winds. Point up to him that Jesus referred to the lives of men. Ask him if it isn't better to build life on a solid foundation. He will agree. Then show him that Christ is the only sure foundation for his life (1 Cor. 3:11). When he has admitted this, then hasten to tell him how to build by faith and repentance on this eternal foundation.

The lawyer.—After a few minutes of pleasant conversation, the soul-winner may ask the lawyer if just anybody is able to practice before the Supreme Court of the United States. Then, of course, the lawyer will reply by pointing out that only those who have been recognized by the Chief Justice are permitted thus to plead at that court.[10]

Then the soul-winner may point out to him that there is a Supreme Court of the universe. He may point out that Christ will be the judge on the last day, that only Christ is recognized by the God of the heavens as having the right to plead in that court. Ask him kindly and tenderly if he has placed his case in the hands of the Christ.

If he should seek to evade the issue by saying he has no case, then you will point out to him that all have sinned and come short of the glory of God and that the penalty of death is upon all sinners; therefore, he does have a case. Show him that he is guilty of sin; he has rejected Christ and therefore he is guilty of the greatest of all sins. It is imperative that someone should represent him before the court of the universe, and no one except the person in authority can do this. Therefore, it is important that he secure the services of Christ. Then you will hasten to show him that through simple faith and repentance Christ becomes his intercessor (1 John 1:9).

The soul-winner must use tact. "Behold, I send you forth as sheep in the midst of wolves: be ye therefore wise as serpents, and harmless as doves. But beware of men: for they will deliver you up to the councils, and they will scourge you in their synagogues" (Matt. 10:16–17). From this statement of Christ we learn that tact means "touch." It is saying the right thing with a great amount of common sense. It is an effective touch. It is illustrated in the excellent bedside manners of a good doctor. He is gentle and knows just what to say. He says only enough to give the patient a lift. He does not enter the bedroom abruptly and unmindful of the patient's condition. He knows the condition of the patient, and he wants him to recover. His manners are harmless, and his words are wise. Since the word "tact" carries the idea of "touch," it is more untactful not to begin at all than to begin awkwardly. Only the person who is willing to begin will learn tact.

One must learn to be tactful. This he will do by studying the approach of others; by praying for wisdom in persuading men; by doing. The best way to learn to do anything is by doing. Nothing may take precedence over experience. Some by nature will be more tactful than others, but all may acquire it.[11]

One may begin by simply presenting a tract to an individual. Dr. John Caylor of the Home Mission Board used to say often, "It is well to have something in your hands, something in your head, and something in your heart." And he would always say that it is excellent to have a good tract in your hand; when someone answers the door, present the tract to him and tell him who you are, what church you are from, and seek to get entrance into the home. As the tract is presented, it will give the soul-winner a chance to say to the person out of experience and wisdom what is on his heart. If he has had a heart experience with God, then it will be possible for him to reveal to the individual his need and the way to have it satisfied.

It is often well to present the tract as you present yourself, then reach and take the tract back and hold it in your hands while you talk to the individual and while you read the Scriptures to him, so that his attention will not be divided. He may try to read some of the paragraphs of the tract while you are talking with him and thus not get the content of either. When the conversation is finished, whether the individual has been won to Christ on that particular visit or not, return to him the tract so that, if he has not been won, he may study the tract for himself. If he did accept Christ as his Saviour, then a close study of the tract will reveal to him more perfectly what has transpired in his own heart.

Let the soul-winner locate a great need in the life of the prospect which is recognized as a need by the prospect. Dr. Sweazey points out that everyone will not have a hunger for God, but all will have a longing of some sort that may be used.[12] Philip won the Ethiopian on the road to Gaza by beginning with something which was in the heart of the Ethiopian and recognized by him as a great need. He was returning from Jerusalem, where he had worshiped in the Temple, and yet it was still not clear to him as he read the account in Isaiah of the coming of the Messiah. He did not understand. There was a hunger in his heart. There was a need in his soul which no religion and no ceremonies had satisfied. Philip began at the passage of Scripture which he was reading and at the point of concern which was in his heart and preached Christ to him, and the Ethiopian accepted Christ as Saviour.

There is a great need in the life of almost every individual, and this need is recognized. It may not be readily admitted, but it is recognized. And if through conversation and through repeated visits the soul-winner is successful in finding out what it is, it will give him entrance to the soul of that individual. It may be a problem concerning the home; it may be a social difficulty; it may be a moral complex; it may be a fear of current events and the trends of the times. Whatever it is, the soul-winner, with the help of the Holy Spirit, can successfully use it to unlock man's soul.

Chapter 5

Techniques of the Master Soul-Winner

A careful study of the interviews of Jesus will reveal the methods which he employed in the operation of soul-winning. He approached all classes of people. His personal evangelism ran the gamut. He dealt with people from the lowest stratum of society to the folks at the very top. He won religious leaders who were held in high esteem by the local citizens. He took time to win blind beggars. He was as careful to win scarlet women who lived in hopeless surroundings. He never failed to use the proper approach. He followed the approach with spiritual instructions and clinched the interview with a gripping appeal. Jesus was almost always direct in his approach and generally went out of his way and over conventional lines to contact people. Only a few times did they approach him. He was alert to his opportunities.

We shall only have space to look closely at one of his great interviews with the lost. All of these interviews are so intriguing and so different that it is difficult to select one as an example. It is our hope that the student will become interested enough to study all the other interviews of Jesus for himself. Each one is a masterpiece in soul-winning and will give insight to the present-day disciple of Christ.

We have chosen the interview with the scarlet woman at the well of Jacob (John 4:1–22).

Factors Which Determine the Approach

The place.—It took place at a well side one mile outside Sychar, which was ancient Shechem. Today the city is called Nablus. It was then possibly a town of five thousand, but now it is a city of over sixty thousand souls. The place was Jacob's well. It is between Mt. Ebal on the east and Mt. Gerizim on the west—the Mountain of Curses and the Mountain of Blessings, respectively. The well of Jacob is one of the indisputable localities connected with the Bible. Twenty centuries before Jesus sat on the curb of the well, it was digged by Jacob. Almost twenty more centuries have passed, and the well is still there, and the water still as plentiful, as clear, and as cold.[1] The writer was there recently and stood by the rim of the well and drank a cup of cold, clear water drawn from the well by a priest who ministers to the small Catholic church which has built a shelter over the sacred spot.

The remarkable thing about the place is that it was located in Samaria. The Jews would not walk across the soil of Samaria. En route to Galilee from Judea they would travel north until they came to the border of Samaria, and then they would turn east and cross the Jordan and turn north again and go up the eastern bank of the river until they had passed Samaria. When they had passed Samaria, they would cross the Jordan and go into Galilee. These Samaritans were hated by the Jews because they were a mixed breed. They had intermarried with their captors, the Assyrians, some seven hundred years before Christ. Jesus was free from such scruples. He could pass through Samaria with love in his heart for them rather than contempt.

The background of the woman.—She was a Samaritan. This posed a race problem. It was incorrect for a man to speak to a woman in public. It was unthinkable to speak to a Samaritan woman. The gulf between Jesus and the woman was doubly deep. It was forbidden by custom and frowned upon by racial conventions. Jesus was oblivious of the artificial distinctions held by the races.[2] He ignored the gulf which separated man from man. All men, irrespective of race, were equal in the eyes of the Master. Jesus by his actions here at Jacob's well condemned the cruel conventions of human society forever.

Her social status was of significance. She was a social outcast. She had made serious mistakes. Her social environment was, no doubt, conducive to social sin. She was, doubtless, poor, and had often been cold and hungry. Her training in the home was likely inadequate. Real love was a foreign element to her. These things all put together exposed her to a scarlet life.

One's social background and environment often set the course of one's life. To know this will give the soul-winner an understanding approach. No one is excused for his sins, but no one is won by those who do not take into consideration why these people are guilty of certain sins. When the woman came to the well at the sixth hour, Jesus knew that this in itself marked her as a scarlet one. She avoided coming at the regular hour to shun the vicious and condemning glances of the other women. Women fear the slights and criticisms of each other more than anything else. Jesus saw on her face a fading beauty, a shade of sadness and disappointment.[3] Sin makes one sad. The face is the index of one's life. All who have fallen to easy virtue have been disappointed. Fleshly gratification in a life directed by impulses brings disappointment and disgust.

As to religious background, she had none of the righteousness of God, but was steeped in traditional pride. To this day the greatest single hindrance in Palestine is traditionalism. All classes there have the religious pride and a religious consciousness but no clear conception of God and no sense of personal relation to him. The woman knew the distinctions between the Jews and the Samaritans and all the religious arguments (John 4:20).

The disposition of the soul-winner.—Jesus was weary (John

4:6). The disciples had gone into Sychar to buy food. Jesus relaxed there by the well, looking up on the two historic mountains and remembering that Jacob and Joshua and other great leaders had gazed upon these mountains. He remembered also that mighty transactions had taken place here.

As he relaxed, a woman approached the well to draw water. He was tired. He might have excused himself from speaking on the ground that he was weary, and, besides, it was not proper to speak to a Samaritan woman. The heart of our Lord burned for every lost soul. He was never too exhausted to take advantage of an opportunity. He "must needs go through Samaria" (John 4:4). He had a purpose in passing this way. This was the key to his purpose. Often a great revival begins with the salvation of one soul. Many a revival has failed to materialize because the evangelist was not alert to his personal responsibility.

Jesus was natural in his approach. He was thirsty, and she had access to plenty of water. He did the natural thing. He was very simple. He was never complex. His attitude was correct. He did not look down upon the woman. He got down on her level without compromising with her sin. His natural and easy conversation led her to converse freely with him although he was a Jew.

He was humble—humble enough to get down to her level and talk heart to heart with her, but he did not quail or compromise when points of doctrine were raised. When she referred to the places of worship, Jesus quickly but tenderly replied: "Ye worship ye know not what: we know what we worship: for salvation is of the Jews. But the hour cometh, and now is, when the true worshippers shall worship the Father in spirit and in truth" (John 4:22–23). To be humble is to lose nothing of one's greatness. Even as Jesus spoke in gracious humility to her, she felt the sweep of his greatness and thought him at first to be a prophet (v. 19). Before the interview ended, she embraced him as the Messiah (v. 29).

The Approach

Jesus began at a point of interest. He began with the things she was momentarily concerned with. He began with something she knew about. He began by asking her for a drink of water (v. 7). Jesus knocked on the door of her heart.[4] As the clear, cold, fresh water splashed over the sides of the bucket and cooled the tips of her fingers, it was in the center of her attention. He could merely have remarked about the water from the ancient well, but he did a far more impressive thing. He said, "Give me to drink" (v. 7). That obligated him to her.

This is wisdom in soul-winning. A young pastor won more than half of the men in an oil field town by using this method. They looked on him at first as an upstart fresh from school who had a few sermons to hurl at them. They dodged him on the street. He went out in the oil fields and began to climb upon the base of the derricks and shake hands with men who had oily hands. At first they would say, "Excuse me, preacher, my hands are greasy." He would reply: "That doesn't matter at all. Come on, shake! The same soap that cleanses your hands will cleanse mine." He would ride on the rough, greasy wagons and trucks with the "roughnecks."

It was not long until they began to remark to each other: "That preacher doesn't think he's any better than we are. He is one of us." Soon they were coming to church, and within a half dozen years he had won the most of them to Christ.

Jesus refused to argue with the woman. She brought up the race question: "How is it that thou, being a Jew, askest drink of me, which am a woman of Samaria?" (v. 9). Some think that her reply was given in good nature, saying: "Yes, that's the way with you Jews. You won't have any dealings with us Samaritans until you need something. Then you do not hesitate to ask." [5] It is more likely that in all seriousness she expressed surprise that he, being a Jew and familiar with their prejudices and customs, should ask a favor of her. Jesus ignored the remark and made a statement which laid the foundation for spiritual instructions.

The soul-winner must learn from this example that it is wisdom to keep the emphasis on the great positive truths and never to be beguiled into chasing negatives. Subsequently, when Jesus moved closer to her heart and interposed the personal note, she tried to switch from the personal to the conventional and theological. She injected religious prejudice to move the attention from herself to a doctrinal issue. In dealing with a lost soul, there is only one step to controversy from any point in the interview. The experienced winner will never take that step.

Jesus moved deftly from the material to the spiritual. Jesus replied, "If thou knewest the gift of God, and who it is that saith to thee, Give me to drink, thou wouldest have asked of him, and he would have given thee living water" (v. 10). There are three explosive expressions in that statement.

"If thou knewest the gift of God" revealed her spiritual blindness to the unmerited favors of God and her unawareness of the nearness of God. She could prattle glibly about customs, disputed places of worship, and theological differences, but the presence of God was foreign to her. Being unaware of the nearness of God, she was blind to the knocking of spiritual challenges. The "gift of God" to which Jesus referred was eternal life.[6] Paul said later, "But the gift of God is eternal life through Jesus Christ our Lord" (Rom. 6:23).

"If thou knewest" is a sad commentary on much of human life. Only recently the writer passed within a hundred yards of ancient Bethel, north of Jerusalem. The guide did not mention it, and the writer was oblivious of it until he had gone from the area. What a spiritual joy it would have been to bow and pray on the soil of old Bethel! Often destiny stands before one's door and nods, then passes on unrecognized and unnoticed. It walks by in sorrow. It glistens in the tears of that little mother who loved you and toiled for you, but you wouldn't see it. It might have reached out for you from the eyes of the wife who loved you so, but it eluded your dull grasp. This woman stood near eternal life and its very origin.

The second explosive expression is, "and who it is that saith to thee, Give me to drink." Here before her stood God. Here speaking to her was the promised Messiah. Here was the dream of the prophets. Abraham longed to see Jesus' day. Every prophet and wise leader in Israel prayed to behold him. With the King of kings the scarlet woman held private conversation unawares.

The third utterance and the one which captured her attention was "living water." Jesus had planted her feet solidly on spiritual ground. She was not yet aware of it and was even oblivious of the meaning of "living water." She was still thinking of the material. She said: "Sir, thou hast nothing to draw with, and the well is deep: from whence then hast thou that living water? Art thou greater than our father Jacob, which gave us the well, and drank thereof himself, and his children, and his cattle?" (vv. 11–12). Her question was completely literal, revealing her failure to understand what he meant.

At the same time, she gave expression to a magnificent truth. Jesus had no visible instrument with which to draw. He did not rely on practices common to man to administer his benefits to people.[7] Jesus had made his approach. He had her attention. The contact was established. His prospect was at sea in every respect, and it was time to impart instructions.

Christ Instructs a Thirsty Soul

Jesus began with physical thirst and led to soul thirst. Jesus replied: "Whosoever drinketh of this water shall thirst again: But whosoever drinketh of the water that I shall give him shall never thirst; but the water that I shall give him shall be in him a well of water springing up into everlasting life" (vv. 13–14).

He taught her by analogy. He instructed the woman that "the living water" was spiritual and would have its springs

within one. It was not physical and could not be had by drawing it from some human or natural source.

He instructed her through contrast. He contrasted the effects
of physical water with "living water." Living water would
quench thirst forever; physical water would satisfy only temporarily. He linked living water with the "gift of God," to
which he had previously referred. He came out now and
plainly called it "eternal life."

She at first saw only the surface of his meaning and that
which applied directly to her physical and social needs. She
was a normal sinner. She was just as slow to see the deeper
meanings, but not more so than the average modern sinner.
Like a hungry trout, she struck quickly at the element in his instructions which met her immediate and temporary need. She
said, "Give me this water, that I thirst not, neither come hither
to draw" (v. 15). His words had intrigued her. Somehow, she
thought he could give her a strange water that would meet her
needs. She wanted her thirst curbed forever, but, most of all,
she desired never to come to the well again. This would be a
longed-for freedom—freedom from the noonday toil, but, primarily, freedom from the gaze and criticism of the cynical and
unsympathetic women of the village.

"Give me this water" was a happy response to the approach
of Christ. He began by asking her for a drink; now she was
saying, "Give me this water." His contact had been successful.
He had got her attention and had controlled the conversation,
and now she was obligated to him by her request. This is wise
soul-winning.

His instructions at this point became personal in order to
convict. There will be no conviction for sins until the truth is
pointed at the heart. Jesus said to her, "Go, call thy husband,
and come hither" (v. 16). He did this to reveal the woman to
herself. One may casually realize he is wrong in his life, but it is
often necessary that the curtains be pulled and that the person
look squarely at himself.

Jesus did not accuse her.[8] Accusation is the work of Satan. It is never the work of God or the evangelist. When God's people accuse others, they are doing the work of Satan and not the work of Jesus. This woman would have resented it if Jesus had said, "You are a prostitute." He did not bluntly reprove her or lash out at her for her dereliction. There was a better way, and he found it. He was as adroit in his instructions as he was in his contact.

To recognize a wrong habit is essential before it can be abandoned. The soul-winner must lead the guilty to recognize his wrong. He will not name it, but he will be used of the Holy Spirit to reveal it. Jesus was compelled to lead her to see her innermost need. Up to now she had seen her need only as physical and social, but it went deeper; it was moral and spiritual. It was a soul need. It was more than the burning effect of condemnation; it was the need for soul redemption. Subsequently, when she had been redeemed inwardly, she sought the public gaze to point the citizens of her town to the Saviour. Jesus was forced to lift her emphasis from superficial needs to the real need of the heart.

No doubt she floundered in her mind before she replied to Jesus. To mention that word "husband" was to prick her conscience. It struck hard at her vital relation to life. She admitted, "I have no husband" (v. 17). It was at this stage an admission and not a confession. Conviction was not ripe enough yet to produce confession. The reply of Jesus made an indelible impression on her. It later became the basis of her evangelistic invitation.

Jesus replied, "Thou hast well said, I have no husband: For thou hast had five husbands; and he whom thou now hast is not thy husband: in that saidst thou truly" (vv. 17–18). His ability to recognize her for what she was revealed no special insight, but when he told her details about her past and hit accurately her present, she was stunned.

It is doubtful whether she was dull or unimaginative, but

her reply revealed that she was ordinary. She was a part of her age. She was slow to recognize him as the Messiah, but she felt that he was a prophet. He knew her as well as if he had lived in Sychar all his life. Being a stranger and knowing her as he did was a puzzle to her. There was just one answer: he must be a prophet.

Again, it is clear that she was a normal sinner, because she tried to switch from the personal to the conventional. She added, "Our fathers worshipped in this mountain; and ye say, that in Jerusalem is the place where men ought to worship" (v. 20). She was trying to do one of two things, or both: she either was trying to focus the center of attention on Christ and on his position, or she was trying to switch the attention to a convention or a doctrine that was easily disputable. The average sinner will immediately turn the discussion to hypocrites in the church or to the question of which church is right. This trick is as old as the woman of Samaria. Christ was not detoured. The soul-winner must not be sidetracked. It is never necessary to answer related questions. The one prime question which must be answered is the relation of the sinner to God. If he can be led to accept Christ as Saviour, he will be born into the family of God. When that is settled, all other questions can be easily answered.

The Appeal

The Master Soul-Winner had finished his instructions, and was ready to make the appeal. He brushed aside the question about the place and form of worship and taught her that the mode of worship took precedence over the place and form. He said: "But the hour cometh, and now is, when the true worshippers shall worship the Father in spirit and in truth: for the Father seeketh such to worship him. God is a Spirit: and they that worship him must worship him in spirit and in truth" (vv. 23–24). These were profound words. This was some of the highest revelation he had yet given.

He appealed to her on the basis of the nature of God. All evangelism grows out of the nature of God rather than the nature and need of man.[9] God is a Spirit, and is not confined to an elevated altar in the mountains or to a sheltered one in Jerusalem. God is accessible to all and may be contacted in any place or in any country.

More important than that was the fact that he must be worshiped in spirit. The condition of the heart was primal in worship. "But the hour cometh" referred to the teaching in her religious background. He was saying, "You expect an hour to come when it will be decided either in favor of Jerusalem or Mt. Gerizim, but I remind you that the time is here when the place of worship will appear insignificant in comparison to the person and kind of worship rendered."

"Ye worship ye know not what" (v. 22). The Samaritans worshiped the god of the land (2 Kings 17:27–33) as a local deity, but God is universal.[10] Ignorance is the death of devotion. One cannot long worship God ignorantly. He must know whom and what he is worshiping, or his devotion will disintegrate into idolatry.

True worship consists less of bodily exercise and more of divine power. The worship of the Christian is no longer typical. The legal services were "figures of the true" (Heb. 9:3–24). The question of importance is not where one worships as much as how he worships. Since God is a Spirit, one does not perform the act of worship unless he worships in spirit, nor does he receive the benefits of devotion.

He appealed to the woman on the basis of his Messiahship. If one does not accept Christ as the Son of God, he cannot be saved. Salvation is contingent upon one's confidence in Christ as the Messiah. His explanation of God and the mode of worship led the woman to a full realization of the spiritual emphasis which Jesus was giving.

She said, "I know that Messias cometh, which is called Christ: when he is come, he will tell us all things" (v. 25).

She would withhold any decision until the Messiah came. What Jesus had said sounded correct to her, but she would respond to such deep instructions only from the Messiah. That was exactly what Jesus wanted her to say. He quietly announced to her, "I that speak unto thee am he" (v. 26). This was the clearest revelation regarding himself that Jesus ever gave to anyone. He was not this emphatic with John the Baptist (Matt. 11:4-5). He refused such full-orbed revelation to the religious leaders of the Jews when they politely asked him, "If thou be the Christ, tell us plainly" (John 10:24).

Many would have felt that this audience was unworthy of such revelation. Jesus did not wait for great occasions and dramatic moments to give forth his greatest revelations. Any and all were considered worthy of his best. Any audience is worthy of the best the soul-winner has to give. Neither the size nor the type of the audience makes any difference. The minister will be honest and faithful enough to give out with his best on all occasions. This woman was a most unlikely prospect and far from fertile soil for mighty revelation. In the eyes of the Master Soul-Winner, it was the golden moment for a display of the best which he had. He has given us a deathless example.

Results of the Interview

Jesus was not disappointed in his expectations. The woman left her waterpot and went rejoicing into the city to bear witness to the saving power of Christ.

The disciples were critical. When the disciples returned and saw him talking with a Samaritan woman, they marveled. They said nothing to him, but merely glanced at each other with telltale expressions. Silent criticism is the sharpest.

The woman became a witness. She went into the city and said to the people, "Come, see a man, which told me all things that ever I did: is not this the Christ?" (v. 29). This was a new kind of sermon. It was an invitation; it was a plea to "come, see." The citizens of the city strangely responded because they saw a change in the woman. She was in no way the same person. Many believed as a result of her brief witness. They trusted Christ before they ever saw or heard him. They believed because of the woman (v. 39).

A great revival ensued (vv. 40–41). The city came out to him. They urged him to remain and preach. He remained two days, and "many more believed because of his own word" (v. 41). No eyes are as blessed of God as the eyes of the soul-winner. The soul-winner sees divine life meet the currents of ordinary life and transform it into the glorious products of redemption. What dynamics we deal with! What miracles unfold before our eyes!

Chapter 6

How to Win the Anxious

The anxious is one who is concerned about his soul's salvation. He has heard enough of the gospel to be interested, but he has not believed with his heart. He is hungry hearted and longs for relief, but needs guidance. He may readily admit that he has done all he knows to do and has not found peace with God. He may complain that he has held up his hand in revival services and has even signed a decision card, but it does not satisfy. This person is ready to be won to Christ.

A knowledge of how to deal with the interested is basic in soul-winning. It is the state to which all must arrive before they can be saved. The preoccupied, the doubter, the Jew, *et alii.*, must come to a deep concern. When they are concerned, from that point on the winner of souls will deal with them just as he does with the anxious. This is largely why we start with the concerned.

We begin with the concerned also because there are many who are in this classification. A surprisingly large number of lost people are either vitally or remotely interested. Many a man has lost his soul, not because he was not concerned but because no one told him about Jesus.

The anxious remains lost because he is ignorant of the way to God. The eunuch was anxious about his soul. He went all the
74

way to Jerusalem to worship as a Judaistic proselyte. He even read the holy Scriptures. When Philip asked him, "Understandest thou what thou readest?" (Acts 8:30), the eunuch replied, "How can I, except some man should guide me?" (Acts 8:31).

Thousands are crying out in their hearts for someone to guide them. The Philippian jailer was convicted, and cried out, "Sirs, what must I do to be saved?" (Acts 16:30). Paul was there to answer, "Believe on the Lord Jesus Christ, and thou shalt be saved, and thy house" (Acts 16:31). The tragedy of today is that thousands cry out, "What must I do?" in their hearts and no one comes to answer.

Cornelius was an anxious seeker. He was a good man; he was devout (Acts 10:2). He feared God and prayed to God. He gave gifts to people. He fasted often (Acts 10:30) and even received a vision from God. He sent for the soul-winner to come and assist him. He sent men to Joppa to bring Peter to talk to him (Acts 10:33). As is often true, God had more trouble with the soul-winner than with the sinner. The sinner was persistently seeking, but the soul-winner was sleeping behind fictitious conventions and waiting for God to bowl him over with a vision. When Peter was convinced that God was leading, he came cautiously to Caesarea.

Peter's approach was a sound one. He began by asking Cornelius certain questions and then proceeded to give him vital instructions. The situation was so ripe that Peter did not have a chance to finish his sermon before the Holy Spirit was able to do his work (Acts 10:44). Rather often the anxious is converted before the appeal is made.

The Approach to the Anxious

The approach which Christ used with Nicodemus, who was an interested soul, is classic.

The determining factor in the approach to Nicodemus was the situation.

Nicodemus came by night (John 3:2). It is not likely that he was afraid of popular opinion, for ranking Jews were coming all along to Christ.[1] It is not likely that he was too busy to come at any other time. It is possible that it was at this hour that conviction became so great that he did not care to wait until the next morning for the interview. He felt that he must come immediately to the Master. This deep concern was the determining factor in the approach.

The profession and background of Nicodemus helped to compose the determining factor of the approach. Nicodemus was scholarly; he was a student of the Talmud and of the Old Testament.[2] His scholarship took on a spiritual turn. He had a messianic expectation. His knowledge of the Old Testament and his knowledge of what Jesus was doing at that time led him to the conviction that Jesus could well be the Messiah. The life and ministry of Jesus had convicted the spiritually minded student that Jesus fulfilled the clear messianic predictions of the prophets. This whetted his desire to seek a personal interview with Jesus.

The approach was direct. Jesus did not seek Nicodemus, but Nicodemus sought him.

Jesus was very cautious and listened patiently to the seeking heart. Listening is often an excellent technique. Jesus learned four vital things by listening to the conversation of Nicodemus.

He learned that Nicodemus was susceptible. Nicodemus began by calling Jesus "Rabbi." This was the highest honor he knew to give Jesus. He was, therefore, not narrow and prejudiced, but had an open mind.

He learned that Nicodemus was on the right track: "We know that thou art a teacher come from God" (v. 2). He did not think Christ to be an impostor or an insurrectionist. He believed Jesus to be some great one sent from God.

He found that the knowledge of Nicodemus was incomplete. Nicodemus had said, "A teacher come from God" (v. 2). He believed Jesus to be a great teacher who had the power and blessings of God on him. He thought of Jesus as a man who could be the Messiah. He does not say this in words, but he implied it by coming for the interview.

Jesus also learned by listening to Nicodemus that his background was strictly legalistic. Nicodemus was clinging eagerly to the national privilege. He felt, as many did, that if one was a Jew, that was sufficient and he would be saved anyhow. Jesus exploded this idea when he said, "That which is born of the flesh is flesh; and that which is born of the Spirit is spirit" (v. 6). The religious background and teaching of Nicodemus had also led him to depend heavily upon sacramental purification, temple offerings, slaying of lambs, etc. But when Jesus instructed him that salvation was a matter of the new birth—a radical spiritual, individual change—he began marveling, for such teaching took the heart out of all of his previous religious instructions. Jesus was able, therefore, to lead the great ruler to see that salvation was a personal matter between himself and God.

Jesus went to the heart of the problem. Jesus told him that "Except a man be born again, he cannot see the kingdom of God" (v. 3). Jesus began his approach by saying, "Verily, verily." This expression was equivalent to "Amen." It was a very strong emphasis placed at the beginning of a statement to stress the importance of the thing which was about to be said. It was a warning of a forthcoming statement of great magnitude, and that which followed was shocking: "Except a man be born again, he cannot see the kingdom of God." Jesus was saying that it is not enough to stand off and admit that Jesus is from God. He must let the life of God, which was in Christ, enter him to re-create him. He must begin all over again. Nicodemus could not understand it; it startled him. He was not being evasive when he asked, "How can a man be born when he is old?" (v. 4). To him the problem was real and the question unanswerable. He had been brought up in the tradition of the Jews. He was a Pharisee. He was a ruler of the Jews. Why should he go back to the very beginning and start all over? He was born of good stock and had the best in religious training, and to tell him that he must be born anew was revolutionary. He had depended on things and ceremonies to save him, but salvation was a spiritual transaction. It involved his relation to a person; that person was Christ.

Begin with the concerned by pointing up Christ as the Saviour. Show how Christ "gave himself for our sins, that he might deliver us from this present evil world, according to the will of God and our Father" (Gal. 1:4). It would be well to take a few passages, one at a time, and slice them up into thin slices like a loaf of bread and feed them to the hungry inquirer. Galatians 3:13 is an excellent verse to use in this manner: "Christ hath redeemed us from the curse of the law, being made a curse for us: for it is written, Cursed is every one that hangeth on a tree."

Christ had redeemed us. Let the inquirer read the verse through slowly as it is written. Then have him read it again, placing *me* instead of *us* in the sentence. Then ask, "Whom hath he redeemed?" Have him answer, "Me."

From what hath he redeemed us? Let him read, "the curse of the law."

Then ask, "How has he redeemed us?" Let him read, "being made a curse for us." Explain to him that we are justly under the curse of the law because we are guilty of the law, but that Christ has redeemed us from that curse by absorbing the blows of the curse in our stead.

Help the inquirer to see why Christ can save from sin. He probably understands by now that Christ is our sin-bearer, but he may not know why. Since he does not know why, it may confuse him. At this point, show him why Christ is able to save us from our sins. He knows that he needs a Saviour; you have told him that Christ is that Saviour; but he must realize that Christ is able to save him.

There are two reasons why Christ is able to save, the first being that he died for our sins. He poured out his blood a libation for sins. We have, therefore, redemption through his blood (Col. 1:14). Because of the shed blood of Christ, sinners are justified (Rom. 5:19). Through his death it became possible for men to be reconciled to God. "And without shedding of blood is no remission" (Heb. 9:22).

The word "remission" is very interesting and revealing. It means to send away, to carry out of sight. Its meaning originates in a redemptive act in the Old Testament. In connection with the Day of Atonement two goats were chosen and lots were cast. By this method one goat was chosen to be offered for a sin offering, and the other goat, called the scapegoat, was carried by fit hands into the wilderness outside the camp and released, never to return to the camp (Lev. 16:10). He symbolically carried away the sins of the people. This was only a symbol. Christ was in reality to carry the sins away. "Christ died for our sins according to the scriptures" (1 Cor. 15:3).

This was essential, but, as Dr. Torrey points out, it is only half the gospel.[3] The other half is just as vital: "He rose again the third day" (1 Cor. 15:4). This is the rest of the gospel. If he had not arisen from the dead, his death would not have atoned for sins.

In the second place, therefore, Christ is able to save from sin because "he ever liveth to make intercession for them" (Heb. 7:25). Death is the fruit of sin. Christ has proved that he has power over death, because he was raised from the dead. Is it therefore incredible to believe that he who has power over death can also give us victory over sin, the cause of death? Jesus is not only alive forevermore (Rev. 1:18), but "He ever liveth to make intercession" for us (Heb. 7:25). One who has demonstrated power over sin and death, and who is alive and stands before the throne of God ceaselessly for us, can redeem us.

Instructions for the Anxious

Show him why he is disturbed about his soul. The concerned is often deeply disturbed. He feels that God does not know about him and certainly does not love him. The witness may sharpen his attention by asking him if he is at any time deeply troubled about his soul condition.[4] He likely will reply in haste, "Sure, I am." Then ask him, "Why do you think you are troubled, and who do you think is troubling you?" The chances are he does not know and may give one of many answers. He may complain that his conscience troubles him.

At this point, inform him that it is not his conscience but that you can show him who it is and why. Then have him read John 16:8: "And when he is come, he will reprove the world of sin." Tell him that his troubled feeling is conviction for sins. Tell him that God has convicted him to help him see and feel the need of soul salvation. When the winner has convinced the concerned that God is convicting him and that God loves him and has provided a Saviour, then the winner is ready to give the second part of his vital instructions.

Tell him how to receive Christ. The witness may tell him to believe, but he may not know what it means to believe. Let him read John 1:12 all the way through once. Then have him read it slowly again: "As many as received him. . . ." Stop him at that point and ask him what did they do. He will reply, "They received him." He will continue reading, ". . . to them gave he power to become the sons of God." Stop him again and ask him what did they become. He will answer, "They became sons of God." Then ask what made them sons of God. He will very likely be able to answer immediately, but if he hesitates, point out that it was the power of God.

Then go back and ask slowly and distinctly three different questions, taking them one at a time. The questions, in order, are, first, "What makes one a son of God?" Take time to review the statement that it is the power of God. Then ask the second question, "When does one become a son of God?" Show him that the clear answer is when he receives Christ. The third question is, "How does one receive Christ?" Then have him read the answer, ". . . even to them that believe on his name"

(John 1:12). This will help him know what faith is and how it works.

Many times the sinner will exclaim, "Oh! I did not know that it was this simple." He will often add, "Why, I can receive him, for I do believe." When he has believed, show him what he now possesses. Read slowly John 3:36; then have him read it: "He that believeth on the Son hath everlasting life." When he has finished reading it, ask him, "What do you have?" The light will break through, and he will realize that he has eternal life because he has received Christ by faith.

The way Jesus led Nicodemus to embrace the simple faith that saves is one of the clearest examples in all the Bible. When Jesus had contrasted the physical birth with the spiritual and emphasized the necessity of the new birth, Nicodemus asked, "How can these things be?" (John 3:9). He literally meant to ask, "What is the basis of the new birth?"

Jesus used an illustration which was familiar to the ruler of Israel. He recalled the time when the Israelites were bitten by the fiery serpents in the wilderness (Num. 21:9). He reminded Nicodemus of how Moses instructed the people to lift up in the camp a brass serpent and instructed those bitten by the snakes to look upon the serpent and be healed. Those who had faith enough to look were healed, and those who did not perished. Then Jesus applied the instructions to Nicodemus. He said, "As Moses lifted up the serpent in the wilderness, even so must the Son of man be lifted up" (John 3:14). He referred to his death on the cross as the basis for salvation. Then he instructed further that "whosoever believeth in him should not perish, but have eternal life" (v. 15). Jesus was saying, "You must look to the crucified Christ and believe for soul salvation just as the Israelites looked to the serpent and by simple faith in God's words were healed."

Jesus went a step further with the inquirer and taught him that back of God's actions on the cross lay the purest motive known to men—love. "God so loved the world" (v. 16). "How can these things be?" They are possible because of the love of God for lost men. "How can these things be?" They are made possible through the death of God's Son on the cross. "How can these things be?" This new relation to God is made real by faith. "He that believeth on him is not condemned: but he that believeth not is condemned already, because he hath not believed in the name of the only begotten Son of God" (v. 18). These were the plain, probing, and simple instructions which Jesus gave Nicodemus to lead him to faith.

The simple faith that saves is illustrated vividly many times in the New Testament. While Jesus ate in the home of a certain Pharisee, a sinful woman came in uninvited. She stood behind Jesus weeping and washed his feet with her tears and wiped them with the beautiful hairs of her head. She anointed his feet with a very costly ointment. Jesus forgave her of her sins (Luke 7:48). She did not know what to do or the polite way to answer the Master's invitation to come to God when she heard him preach, but in tears she threw herself down at his feet before the critical group at the feast. At the feet of Christ she received forgiveness for sins. Her actions constituted a response of faith.

Her attitude is sure to bring salvation, and the soul-winner may point out to the concerned that if he will cast himself down at the feet of Christ, regardless of how much he may understand or may not understand, he will receive the same forgiveness of sin which the woman received at the feast in the house of the Pharisee.

Lead the concerned to confess his sins to God. A certain pastor had been cultivating a hardened sinner for several months and decided that the time had come when he must press him for a decision. The man was a very callous sinner. He was about thirty-five years old. His mother had prayed often for him and had shed many tears in grief. When the pastor entered the outer office, the man's mother, who worked with him, greeted the pastor. The pastor asked her to keep all visitors out of the inner office. After a few minutes of direct and pointed instructions, the pastor asked him if he would kneel for prayer, to which he replied with a vicious curse word and added, "Yes, if it will do any good." Seeing that his reply was out of place, he said, "Excuse the French, preacher; I didn't mean any harm."

The pastor replied: "That is not French; that is the language of your father the devil. But despite such blasphemy, if you will kneel and call on God, he can save you." The preacher was not soft and did not intend to quail before a blasphemer. The man was moved by the pastor's directness and tenderness at the same time. The pastor prayed tenderly for the sinner and then stopped praying and asked him to pray. He said: "I can't pray! I just can't!"

The pastor instructed him to repeat a prayer sentence by sentence after him, and the man did. When he repeated, "I am a sinner," etc., he burst into tears and sobbed out his heart. There is just something about confessing sins that will move a sinner inside. "He that covereth his sins shall not prosper: but whoso confesseth and forsaketh them shall have mercy" (Prov. 28:13).

When the converted man and the pastor walked to the door, the mother ran to them. The pastor turned and said, "Bill, tell your mother what happened." He did not need to, for she knew; she could see it. When a man is converted, it shows in his face; it cannot be hidden. The elderly woman threw one arm around her son and one around the pastor, and they literally wept and shouted for joy.

That pastor went out of that office back upon the streets with the joy bells of heaven ringing in his soul. He could preach the next day with confidence and power. Nothing thrills the soul and nothing stimulates one's ministry like soul-winning. Simple, direct instructions which led to confession enabled God to bring about the miraculous change in the life of the seemingly incorrigible young man.

Chapter 7

How to Win the Indifferent

The indifferent has no genuine conception of spiritual values and no concern for his soul. He sees no need for a Saviour. He is ignorant both of his spiritual needs and of the way to God. Because of his ignorance of spiritual values, he may treat contemptuously the overtures of the soul-winner. He lives aimlessly in the world. He lives here as if he were to live forever.

The writer spoke to an elderly man recently about his soul. He was so indifferent that he brushed the inquiry aside and said: "You travel a great deal and must see many business opportunities. Where could I safely invest a surplus of several thousand dollars?" He only had a few months or possibly years at best on earth but thought and acted as if he had an eternity here. Since he was absorbed in investments, I read to him an excerpt from the Sermon on the Mount: "Lay up for yourselves treasures in heaven, where neither moth nor rust doth corrupt, and where thieves do not break through nor steal: For where your treasure is, there will your heart be also" (Matt. 6:20–21).

Briefly we tried to show him that it was wisdom to prepare not only to live here but to live for eternity. The best one can do in most cases with the indifferent is to get in a sound word here and there. You are not likely to have an opportunity to talk long at a time with them in your first contacts.

84

The Situation

The indifferent is difficult to approach. There are three reasons for this religious unconcern.

The indifferent is preoccupied. He is usually a busy man. He is absorbed in making a fortune. Making money has become an obsession with him. On the other hand, he may be preoccupied with pleasure and worldliness. He is "living it up." His heart is cold toward the spiritual because of fleshliness. He may be dedicated to acquiring an education. In his quest for knowledge he has no time for his soul. He feeds his spiritual hunger, if he has any, with a stone instead of the bread of life. He may even be preoccupied with his home. He wants the best for his family. He bends all his energies in that direction. The vast majority of pursuits which blind his eyes to his spiritual needs are worthy and may be used as a prolific basis for the approach to his soul.

Religious confusion has often produced indifference. Fanaticism often produces distaste for spiritual religion. Unprepared preaching and unscriptural statements confuse and undermine respect for the churches. Small groups of fanatics who speak out of the abundance of their ignorance rather than the Bible do great hurt and increase the growing number of the indifferent.

Worldliness in many churches and church members also contributes to indifference.[1] The selfish living of Christians causes the preoccupied to grow more careless. Dr. Murray W. Downey says, "The reason why there are so many careless sinners is because there are so many careless saints." [2] When the churches are awake and the genuine flame of spirituality burns in the hearts of church members, the unconcerned will be more easily led to a state of concern.

Some Methods of Approach

It is important to have the correct viewpoint. Your point of view will be reflected in your approach.[3] You must have confidence in yourself and in God. You realize that the indifferent is hard but not impossible. If you have confidence, your chances of success are many times more than those of the individual who is fearful and timid about his approach. If you approach the prospect with confidence and consideration, you have nine chances to one that you will be received with the same politeness and confidence. If one is abrupt and impatient, he reflects lack of confidence.

It is wise to put yourself in the prospect's place. If you do, you will not approach him at an inopportune time. Remember, he is very busy. He is absorbed in his pursuits and very jealous of them. If you would win his heart, you will not overlook this fact. Unless you know why he behaves as he does, you will not be able to get inside his confidence. You may begin by saying: "I see you are very busy, and I won't speak with you now. When could you spare five minutes to answer a question?" It will please him to see that you are considerate of his time. He will feel more kindly disposed toward you and your project. He may even suggest that he could spare five minutes now.[4] You will be too wise, however, to take him up on this generous offer. You will answer by suggesting a definite date to return.

The correct approach will secure for you a pleasant response. There are exceptions to the rule. A few will resent any intrusion and will demonstrate a haughty spirit. Do not be discouraged by the few, but remain hopeful for the many. Keep using your approach again and again. It will work in most cases.

The approach must be positive. Anticipate your prospect and know what to say. Familiarize yourself with his type, his problems, and with the Scriptures which fit his case. You will never say, "I am the pastor of a certain church, and I felt impelled to come and see you." Do not say, "I am a member of the church, and we are merely inviting all unchurched to come visit our church." Do not contact the prospect by telephone and then spend your time figuring that he is too unconcerned and does not constitute a "good prospect." The soul-winner with the positive mind will go to see the prospect and make a definite date and go back and face to face seek to make of him a "good prospect."

The positive approach will incorporate certain reasons why one should turn to Christ. Let us give our attention to some of these.

Show the prospect that there are some things that even a busy man cannot be without. Show him the need for eternal security. Remind the preoccupied that he is busy partially because he wants security for himself and his family. Point out that life on earth is brief and that the soul will live forever somewhere. Show him that it is even more essential that shelter and eternal security for the soul be provided. Life here is brief compared with eternity. If security here is so vital that it challenges one's best, what about eternal security? List certain safeguards against mental and social bankruptcy for himself and his family. Show him how Christ has brought security and social stability to thousands of families in all the ages.

If the prospect is preoccupied with worldly pleasures and careless living, show him that genuine Christianity makes for better physical health. Every man longs for his family to have the best of health. Point up to him that worldly living leads to the loss of health and to premature death. Show how one endangers his health by slovenly living. Give examples and quote medical doctors. If he is preoccupied with worldliness, this may be a sobering approach.

Peace of mind is essential to health and prolonged productivity. Point out all the implications, and show him that a proper relation to God in Christ can produce a stable and untroubled mind.

Whatever the approach, do not make it a one-way conversation. Welcome participation from your prospect. Give him a chance to express himself. From his conversation you will know if he is ready for definite instructions. If the approach has been successful, it has produced two essentials: you have been given a good reception, and the prospect has responded favorably. A proper reception and a wholesome reaction are vital.

Agencies Which Produce Concern

Prayer has been used to produce concern. Prayer has a psychological effect when it is uttered in the presence of the sick or the unconcerned. This psychological effect is not the main thing. It is not to be considered unimportant, but if this were the only effect of prayer, it would be better to use something else. The power of prayer goes far beyond this. When prayer is sent up in earnestness to God for an indifferent person, it has often had a remarkable effect. When a number of Christians get deeply concerned for a hardened sinner and many pray privately and in groups for him, he is almost always converted. When concern among Christians becomes so great that the natural result is much prayer, the indifferent is moved.

Sermons empowered by the Holy Spirit produce concern. The gospel is the power of God unto salvation. If one can bring the indifferent under the influence of the gospel, he will be convicted. In a Tennessee town a professed infidel came to church. God had led the pastor to prepare a message on "Life After Death." The message was exactly what the unbeliever needed. In a simple yet profound way it answered some problems which had bedeviled him all his life. The professed infidel was converted. He had been able to shake off all individual approaches, but in a worship atmosphere where the truth was convincingly presented the man was moved in his heart, and his will was captivated by the Christ of the resurrection.

The Bible and religious literature have their part. A very wild and careless young man who would not even attend church came to visit his brother who was a churchman. The brother did not talk to him about his prodigality, but placed some attractively bound books of Mark, Luke, Matthew, and John on the tables and on the shelves in the house. The young man took up one of the beautifully bound Gospels and read it. He read another; and when he left, he took away a pocketful of the little books. The next time the brother saw him, he was converted. A few months later he surrendered to preach and today is one of the most consistently evangelistic pastors of Texas. The power of the written Word of God is amazing. It has often done for the unconcerned what no soul-winner could have done, irrespective of his approach.

Instructions for the Indifferent

Begin with the love of God. The indifferent is so constituted that a realization of the pure love of God may do more to create concern in him than any other type of instruction which the soul-winner may use. The soul-winner may do three things in leading the indifferent to get a complete picture of the love of God.[5]

Take a comprehensive look at the love of God. Read John 3:16 slowly to the person; then have him read it audibly. Tell him that "the world" means all men who are lost. Tell him that it means him. Have him read the passage again, substituting his name for "the world." Then ask him, "What did God's love do for you?" He will answer, "It led God to give his Son for me." Then ask, "To give one's own son to die for you requires a great love, does it not?" He will answer in meditation, "Yes." If he shows no signs of understanding, then continue your cautious instructions at this same angle. However, people are very alert to recognize and appreciate real love.

A woman of ill fame, whose beauty was fading and whose health had broken, visited a downtown mission to get a warm meal and heard a kindly old gentleman tell the story of the love of God. It was a strange story to her. Real love was unknown to her. When the service was over, the elderly preacher spoke tenderly to her and, seeing her physical condition, took her to the home of a kindly Christian woman whom he knew to love the fallen. He obligated himself to pay for her lodging until she recovered her health.

One morning the kind, elderly woman who kept the house came upstairs with a tray of food for the sick girl and, finding her asleep, placed the tray beside her bed and then kissed her on the cheek. It awakened the fallen woman. She was not sure that the older woman had kissed her. She knew that if she had it was a kiss of real love. She knew also that it proved what the elderly minister had said about the pure love of God. She decided to find out. She knew that if the older woman had kissed her, she would probably do it again.

The next morning when she heard the kind woman coming up the stairs with the tray, she pretended to be asleep. The elderly lady set the tray on the table and planted a tender kiss on the fading cheek of the prostitute. A warm thrill permeated the soul and body of the scarlet woman when she realized that the elderly lady really loved her and had planted upon her cheek a kiss of real love. As a result of this, she took Christ as her Saviour. She was won by a gesture of real love—the love of God in the heart of a kindly old Christian woman. All the eloquence and pleading this side of the gates of heaven could not have accomplished what love had done.

Carlyle Brooks has said a thousand times, "Love them for Christ's sake." He does just that. He enters ten thousand homes each year to tell the indifferent the story of God's love. For more than thirty years he has been doing this, and for all this time God has blessed his ministry because he loves the lost.

Point up the purpose of the love of God. Burn into the heart of the listener a passage of Scripture which reveals the purpose of the love of God. It is seen in many passages. We refer to only two.

". . . that whosoever believeth in him should not perish, but have everlasting life" (John 3:16). The purpose of God's love is not selfish. It is to deliver man from perishing and give him eternal life. Show the person that this is why the love of God led him to give his Son as a ransom for many. One does not always need to explain these passages. Often it is best to read them and make no explanation at all. Remain silent and see God work his powerful Word.

A pastor recently visited two middle-aged women whom he had never seen before. In the course of the conversation they expressed their disgust with the doctrine of the resurrection. They spoke of the gruesomeness of the idea. He did not reply; he only sat in silence. He could have shown them that the fact which appeared gruesome to them was the brightest star in the heaven of hope to millions, but he did not. When they had finished their tirade against the glorious doctrine, he opened his Bible and read slowly every word of 1 Corinthians 15, which is the greatest treatise on the doctrine of the resurrection that has ever been written. He made no comment. He did not need to, for the Word of God did its work.

The purpose of the love of God is plainly stated in Romans 2:4: "Or despisest thou the riches of his goodness and forbearance and longsuffering; not knowing that the goodness of God leadeth thee to repentance?" Ask him: "Why has God spared you? Why has God blessed you with health and a degree of prosperity? Why do you suppose that God has been so good to you?" Help him to see that it is because God loves him and because God is patiently trying to lead him to repentance. The indifferent are often slow to see the point. If his answers to the questions are vague or incorrect, have him to go back and reread the passage until he can reply, "To lead to repentance."

Show him, in the third place, the results of despising the love of God: "But after thy hardness and impenitent heart treasurest up unto thyself wrath against the day of wrath and revelation of the righteous judgment of God" (Rom. 2:5). You have shown him that the love of God and God's goodness are to bring him to repentance. Now show him from this Scripture verse the penalty of wilfully rejecting God's love. He is under the just condemnation of God. God's love stays this judgment. A persistent refusal of the love of God will finally bring the wrath of God upon one.

Many have been brought to Christ because of the love of God. One such Christian said, "Fear set me to thinking, but love led me to decide." [6] "The fear of the Lord is the beginning of wisdom." The fear of God is not an end within itself; fear is only the factor which awakens. When fear integrates into a deep reverence for God, it moves one toward God. If the one moved is led to recognize the love and goodness of God, it will help him to decide. The writer heard a little girl in a tent revival in Germany stand up and testify, "God is love." Her testimony would not have been significant but for the fact that her mother had died two weeks before. She knew that God had not taken her mother, but, when death had taken her, God had borne her spirit away for safekeeping. She also recognized that God was standing by her side to be a mother to her in deep sorrow. To her, a Being like this was love and worthy of her love. That day she was publicly standing for God. Love leads to a decision.

Deal with his spiritual condition. If your appeal on the basis of God's love does not reach him, it will be wise to excuse yourself with the understanding that you will see him again if God is willing. Your next instruction should deal with his condition before God. Remember he is hard, and it may require some plain, searching instructions. If one is so hard in heart that the love of God cannot sober him, then it will require a shocking revelation of his spiritual condition. The soul-winner may try three things in this effort.

Tell him plainly that he is a lost soul. Tell him what it means to be lost. Show him that to be lost is more than merely to be outside the fold, but that he is guilty (Rom. 3:19). All the world is guilty before God. Come right out and tell him: "You are a great sinner. In fact, do you realize that you are the greatest sinner?" He will deny this. He will admit that he has sinned but certainly he could not be the greatest sinner. Dr. Torrey suggests the use of Matthew 22:37–38 to startle him into a realization of the magnitude of his guilt.[7] Ask him, "What do you think is the greatest sin?" He may reply, "Adultery or murder."

Then have him read the passage. Ask him, "What is the greatest commandment?" He will read, "Thou shalt love the Lord thy God with all thy heart, and with all thy soul, and with all thy mind." Now ask him, "What is the greatest sin?" He will reply, "A failure to love God." "Do you love God?" He will be forced to say, "No." Then ask him, "What does that make you?" He will realize the magnitude and meaning of his sins. He will see that unconscious omissions born in unbelief are damning sins.

You may even shock him more by saying: "You said a few minutes ago that you thought murder was the greatest sin. Do you know that you are a murderer? Do you know that you have blood on your hands?" He will very likely say: "Why, no, I have never killed anyone. There is no blood on my hands." Have him read, "They are all under sin" (Rom. 3:9). Then have him read Romans 3:23: "For all have sinned, and come short of the glory of God." Use these Scriptures to help him realize that he has sinned, and then point out to him that his sins nailed Christ to the cross. Say to him plainly, "Your sins killed Christ." You may read to him, "Christ died for our sins according to the scriptures" (1 Cor. 15:3). Help him to see from these Scriptures and others that he is guilty of the blood of Christ, that his sins had a part in the crucifixion of Christ, and therefore he is a murderer. Show him that the blood of Christ, God's Son, is on his hands, and that makes him the greatest of all sinners.

Reveal to him the implications involved in his problem. He does not realize the value of his soul and that the loss of it is involved. He does not sense the futility of preoccupation. Explain Matthew 16:26 to him: "For what is a man profited, if he shall gain the whole world, and lose his own soul?" Remember, he is either preoccupied with the pursuits of a great fortune or with playing fast and loose with the world. Help him to see that if he should succeed in gaining the whole world and in the mad rush should lose his soul, it would be a bad bargain. Tell him that the world and the things of the world will perish. They do not endure. Ask him, "Where are the mansions or fortunes of thousands of years ago?" Point out to him that they have perished. Ask him, "Who owned these hundreds of fertile acres eight hundred years ago?" Ask him, "Who will hold title to them eight hundred years from now?" Help him see how fleeting and perishable things are. Then contrast that with the eternal soul. The soul never dies; it lives on forever somewhere. To lose sight of its value and destiny in a blinding effort to gain a little security for life in this temporary world is a lack of foresight unworthy of a man who thinks on his level.

Then go back and show him that no man ever gained the whole world, that no man ever gained a city. Show him that no man was ever able to keep what little he did gain. He can take none of it with him past the mouth of the grave. The soul is so much more valuable than the things of the world that there is no comparison. As Sir William Hamilton stated it, "There is nothing great on earth but man and nothing great in man but his soul." [8] Help your prospect to see the folly of giving all his concern to life here and no consideration to life beyond.

He must be led to realize the penalty for being lost. Instruct him that he is bound for the judgment, as well as for hell. Many are fearful to use this approach, thinking that they may be considered narrow. The soul-winner who would court the applause of this world will never have the incomparable thrill of winning the difficult. It is far better to have the secular world think you narrow than to have many spend eternity in hell because you saved face with contemporary opinion. Are you dedicated to face-saving or to soul-saving? It is our responsibility to warn men of the awful consequences of sin and unbelief.

We must tell the careless that "it is appointed unto men once to die, but after this the judgment" (Heb. 9:27). Explain to him that he must face the judgment. Tell him there is coming a time when the busy, the pleasure lover, the indifferent, and all others must stand before the judgment bar of God. Just as surely as it is appointed unto men once to die, they must also meet the judgment. Picture the judgment to him, using the Scriptures which portray it. Feature how empty and awful it will be to stand there without hope. Show him that God has provided an escape for the consequences of the judgment. Tell him what the provisions are and what to do. This may be as far as you need to go. He may be ready for a decision. If so, press him for an open decision.

If he is not ready, then continue by showing him from the Bible that hell lies ahead also. Explain Matthew 25:46 and Revelation 21:8. Hell is the inescapable destiny of the indifferent and all who wilfully persist in rebellion against God. The Bible teaches the eternal punishment of the wicked. Jesus said, "These shall go away into everlasting punishment" (Matt. 25:46). It was with a heavy heart that he uttered these words. Jesus would not have used such words if they had not been true. Somewhere in the future the good and evil will be eternally separated. If this is not true, then God has lied. The very nature of a merciful and loving God demands it. Apart from justice there is no mercy. It is necessary that the winner of souls warn the careless by using the plain, shocking statement of Jesus. Tell the indifferent that the destiny of the unbeliever is hell. Read and explain the Scriptures which describe the destiny of the damned. Sometimes the unvarnished words of truth will speak when nothing else does.

An entire family and several visitors burned to death in an Oklahoma home a few months ago. If you had passed by and had seen the blaze, knowing that all the occupants were asleep in the house, what would you have done? You would have given an alarm. You would have aroused the sleepers. You would have had no compunction of conscience for causing a little excitement in order to rescue them from the inferno of death. On the other hand, if you had not alarmed the sleepers, you would have been guilty of their death. The responsibility of the soul-winner is great. He holds the destiny of many in his hands. He is accountable to God for the way he uses the Word of God.

Contrast the fruits of a life of indifference to God with those of a life of spiritual rectitude. Show him the advantages of a better life. Future blessings and rewards do not always appeal to this type of person.[9] Help him see that the rewards are received now. He is keenly interested in "now." Tell him that salvation is for "now" and that certain indispensable benefits come immediately. In the first place, he will receive the abundant life. The Christian life is a full life. It produces peace of mind. It enables one to enjoy his possessions. Money is no longer his governor. It becomes a servant. He loses the tensions which produce neurosis and ulcers. A life of trust replaces a life of feverish tension. The preoccupied learns the difference between a Spirit-directed life and one cluttered with things and smothered with care.

In the second place, appeal to him on the basis of his usefulness to others. Show him how Christ could use an enterprising man like himself to bless countless others. Prove it to him by illustrating how Christ has used men of his ability to help thousands of others once they have been saved. The appeal that God can bless many through him has far more weight than the immediate good which he may receive.

Show him how to be saved. At the first sign of concern, proceed immediately to tell him how to accept Christ as Saviour. Help him to realize that it is an easy matter since he is now concerned. Point up how Christ has been patient with him through all of his indifference and has kept tender, loving watch over him. Turn to Revelation 3:20 and read, "Behold, I stand at the door, and knock: if any man hear my voice, and open the door, I will come in to him." Ask him to read the verse.

When he has read, "Behold, I stand at the door," stop him and ask, "Where is Christ standing?" He will answer, "At the door." Ask him, "At the door of whom?" He may answer, "Before my door." If he says, "Any door," then explain that it is before his heart's door. Then let him read, "If any man hear my voice," and stop him and ask, "To whom does that statement refer?" He will reply, "To any man." Then instruct him that it means him or anyone who hears the knock. Let him read, "and open the door," and stop him and ask, "Who opened the door?" He will reply, "Why, the man on the inside." Then tell him how a sinner opens the heart's door to the seeking Saviour. Show him that the Saviour never forces the door. He only knocks; the soul within must unlatch the door. You may explain that this is done by faith and repentance. Tell him that he must be willing or God cannot come into his heart.

Let him read the rest of the sentence: "I will come in to him." Then explain that when Christ comes into the heart one is saved. The transaction is comprised of three simple steps: first, Christ knocks at the door; second, the sinner hears and opens the door; third, Christ comes into the heart. The sinner's part is to hear and open. To hear is manifest in concern, and to open is an act of faith. The Saviour's part is to knock and enter. He knocks to alarm, to get attention, and to create concern. He enters to bring salvation and a reign of peace and power.

Getting a Decision

The soul-winner will miss the point of this discussion if he thinks he should use all the points of instruction given here before he appeals for a decision. He may be able to get a decision after the use of any part of this instruction. It is well to use as little as necessary. He may find it wise to use altogether a different approach than we have suggested and an entirely different type of instruction. All we can do is to outline certain approaches and instructions for the soul-winner. If one has become familiar with the nature of his prospect and has anticipated the basic problems and objections, he will be better prepared to follow the leadings of the Holy Spirit. One should have a planned approach and a planned set of instructions but be prepared to depart from the plan when necessary. If one is led of the Holy Spirit, he will almost always depart from his plan at given points.

Getting a decision is not a separate act. The approach, instructions, and decision are steps in one process. It has often been said that getting a decision is the difference between failure and success in evangelism. If one understands that decision is not separated from all the rest of the process of soul-winning, such an assumption is not dangerous. However, it must be known that one does not win souls by piling up facts and then asking for a decision. One must get a series of agreements throughout his instructions.[10] Get an agreement as often as possible. The decision is an accumulation of the results of effective instructions and appeals.

Do not make the decision; let the prospect decide. Be used of God to create a compelling desire for salvation. Make soul salvation so attractive that the prospect will want it. The unconcerned, like all other sinners, is "dead in trespasses and sins." He is so bound and chained by sin and such a slave to sin that he is not really capable of making a decision without your instructions and without the guidance of the Holy Spirit. But when you have given your instruction and presented your clear appeal, and have been used of God to open the door to him, let him walk through the door. Let it be his decision.

Use the "weighing process" in getting a decision.[11] Getting a decision is easy if your selling process has been successful. The prospect will weigh the ideas in favor of being a Christian, and in contrast he will weigh the ideas against it and make up his mind. If the ideas in favor of Christ have not been convincingly presented, the weight of your appeal will not be enough to tip the scales in favor of a decision in the right direction. The Holy Spirit has been able to use effectively ideas poorly presented. The soul-winner is presuming on God, however, when he fails to put as much study and energy into an effort to win a lost man as a salesman does in selling a product. It is not enough to present the advantages of being a Christian. One must present the disadvantages of continuing in the present course. Remember, his life of sin has brought self-gratification and pleasure to him. He doesn't want to buy Christianity, for it will change things. Show him the advantage of a change and the disadvantage of his present course. Do not be afraid to bring up what he thinks are disadvantages in accepting Christianity. They are in his mind. Bring them up, air them out, and explode them.

The decision has often been made or lost before the time for getting the committal arrives. If one senses that the decision is lost, or that the prospect is not ready to make a decision for Christ, he should stop and wait for another time. If the decision is ready, the closing moment is merely a formality.

It is well to remember, on the other hand, that if the prospect is ready to decide, it will be a colossal mistake to let him put it off. The devil is a person. He is present and doing all he can to prevent a decision in every interview. If the prospect is concerned enough to decide for Christ, do not leave him to cool off. Lead him tenderly to see that now is the time for salvation. The Holy Spirit will dictate to the soul-winner the moment of decision.

Practice the presence of God. When an ordinary salesman goes afield to sell his product, he only has the value of his product to present, plus the weight of his experience and the strength of his personality. The soul-winner has all this and more. He has the presence of God. If the soul-winner does not realize that God is with him and comes to feel that he is battling alone, he is certain to depend more upon himself than upon God. He must learn to depend upon both, and if he recognizes and practices and draws upon the presence of God, he is certain to be far more effective in his approach and instructions.

Chapter 8

How to Win the Jewish People

It will not be possible to define the twentieth-century Jews and their religious beliefs. They have kept their national identity for the most part through the centuries, but their religious ideas have varied with each generation. This is particularly true since the Middle Ages. Jews of the twentieth century in Palestine and in the Diaspora are different from the Jews of any generation, and they differ widely among themselves. In order to have a thorough knowledge of the Jewish people, it will be necessary to make a brief study of the Jews as they are in Israel today and also the Jews in Diaspora.

Who Are the Jewish People?

The Jewish people are no longer a race. They do not consider themselves as a race, but they consider themselves an ethnical group. It is always wise to refer to them as "the Jewish people" and never as "the Jews." Through the centuries they have intermarried with other people. Many people have become Jews by choice. There are many of these people in China, Japan, and other places. For this reason, as well as many others, they would consider themselves an ethnical group. Although some Jews may be direct descendants of Abraham without any mixture of blood, the majority of them are not.

There are slightly less than two million Jews in the land of

100

Israel. There are approximately twelve million Jews in the entire world. Five and one-half million of these people live in America. The Jews who have returned to Israel have gone back with a sense of national solidarity.

The Israeli state has not been set up to give refuge to those who are persecuted and to mete out charity to the unfortunate Jews. Instead, they are interested in building a great state there because they believe it is the only way to endure and to create. They have a keen sense of national solidarity, and this could very well be an open door for Christians to preach Christ to them. The most of the Jews in the land of Palestine believe that the state of Israel is the only answer to anti-Semitism. They believe that to bring the Jews back to their own soil will produce a state of normalcy for them and give them a chance fully and freely to develop their mental and spiritual abilities. They also have a feeling that if they can build a strong homeland, it will create dignity for the Jewish people abroad.

In broad outline, there are three classes of Jews in the land of Israel. There are the orthodox, the liberals, and the nonreligious. The orthodox constitute a minority group which is very strong politically and which has deep religious convictions for the most part. However, it is only fair to say that their religious convictions vary widely even within the orthodox group.

Parliament is made up of a coalition government. The religious block which is constituted largely of the orthodox Jews has gained advantage because of this system, and the laws of marriage, divorce, and inheritance are under their jurisdiction. The nonreligious Jews and the unorthodox who do not adhere to the strict views of the rabbinical Jews are unhappy with it and hold that there is no freedom of conscience or religious liberty in Israel. Rabbinical Judaism bears at this point the seeds of its ultimate defeat.[1]

It might be well to point out that the Talmud and not the law of Moses is responsible for conflict with the plain liberty and full living in Israel. There are more than six hundred laws and commandments in the laws of Moses. The Talmud is the book of religious literature which is largely given to an interpretation of the laws of Moses. The Talmudic interpretations have varied through the years and have enlarged upon the law and become confusing. The Talmud has virtually supplanted the law. It is at this point of departure and human emphasis that a major crisis has arisen with the Jewish layman. The Jewish people in Israel and in the Diaspora realize that the Talmud has been outgrown. The place and emphasis which has been given to the Talmud through the years has laid the foundation for unbelief in the Bible. The dominant place held by rabbinical Judaism in Israel and its continued emphasis upon the Talmud have created a unique problem in the land of Israel.

The nonreligious Jews in Israel, just as the nonreligious Jews in the Diaspora, have no faith in God or in any type of religion. And in many cases they are very bitterly opposed to Judaism.

By "the Jews in Diaspora" we mean the Jews who live outside the land of Israel. More than ten million of the Jewish world population live outside the land of Israel. There are 2,050,000 Jews in New York. The Jews in Diaspora are no longer classified as the descendants of Abraham and described as people with black or brown eyes, curly hair, dark complexion, and curved nose. They may be fair complexioned, blue eyed, and have blond hair and a straight nose. There is almost no distinguishing feature of the Jews living in Diaspora. There are many of the Jewish people living abroad, however, whom one would recognize as Jews by the description which has always been given to them. They have all the physical features, and they are sons of Abraham.

The Religion of the Jewish People

Jewish religious life centers around the home and not around the synagogues.[2] The Jewish religion does not depend upon the synagogue. It may continue to survive forever without the use of worship at the synagogue. Apart from the religion which is practiced and taught in the home, there are several religious groups. They may be classified as the orthodox, reformed, conservative, and reconstructionist.[3]

The orthodox Jews.—The orthodox are few and vary widely. Many of the orthodox rabbis, however, no longer hold to the original conceptions about God, sin, and salvation. A few of the orthodox at home and abroad are strictly rabbinical, but they are in the minority.

The reformed Jews.—Many of the Jews felt that Judaism was too strict and not compatible with the modern system of life. Being dissatisfied with the rigid dietary system and other rites of Judaism, they decided to modify the system. In the modification, they departed widely from the original faith.

The conservative Jews.—Soon after the formation of the group known as the reformed Jews, many became dissatisfied with the extremes of the reform, but they could not be satisfied with remaining under the rigid rule of the rabbinical system. Therefore, they set up a system which was in between; they are called the conservatives.

The reconstructionists.—This particular group of Jewish people looks upon Judaism as an evolving religion. The religious conceptions of this group are little more than a social and cultural way of life.

Great numbers of Jewish people in America and in England are strongly indifferent to all things of a Jewish religious nature. These Jews have no knowledge of the Old Testament and the rabbinical teachings. They care nothing for tradition. They may be in good standing and remain entirely outside the synagogue. Less than a third of the American Jews have any connection with the synagogues. The reason for this decline in religious interest among the Jews in America is fourfold.

There is the background of the Jews in dispersion. In many places in foreign lands the Jews have adopted great changes in their worship services. The Hebrew language was replaced by the language of the people among whom they lived. Sunday services were substituted for Saturday worship in many places, and the forms of worship were altered. These various changes made the modern Jews more open minded and more susceptible to any idea of change. Many of them no longer hold to the ancient dietary and other laws concerning bodily practices. Circumcision is no longer held necessary by the majority of the liberal Jews. Some of them no longer recognize the Talmud as authoritative. Some no longer look for a Messiah. Because of the various changes which they have made to adapt themselves to the society and the age in which they live, there is a background which has made possible the decline in Judaism.

The vague spiritual conceptions which are held by many of the rabbis have laid the foundation for religious decline. Joseph Zeitlin says in his recent book that most American rabbis think that God is "the sum total of forces which make for great intelligence, beauty, goodness, etc." [4] The modern Jews have reduced prayer to little more than a superstitious practice of the past. They calmly hold that it does not bring divine aid. They no longer hold that sin is against God. Their conception of sin is vague. Salvation is no more than an achievement of an integrated personality or co-operation to achieve social progress.[5]

In the third place, the religious decline among Jews in Diaspora is due to the temptations of soft, easy living. In many cases they are prosperous, and have been caught unaware in the grip of worldliness. This is particularly true in America.

In the fourth place, the synagogue no longer holds a strategic place in the Jewish community. The Jews who attend the synagogue do not give it a place of paramount importance in their lives. If such facts as these are known to the soul-winner, he will realize that the Jews are only lost people who need Christ as a Saviour just as the Gentiles do.

The Evangelistic Problem

The Jews are steeped in traditionalism. They possess more traditional pride than almost any people on the face of the earth. They are bound and completely blinded often by tradition. Tradition is one of the greatest hindrances to winning the Jews to Christ.

Prejudice and persecution have served as a great hindrance to evangelizing the Jews. In many nations the Jews have been accepted by one generation in the community in which they lived and then sorely persecuted by the following generation. There is a deep prejudice against the Jews by many Gentiles. The Jews through the centuries have been aware of this prejudice. Unfortunately, many times the Jews have been persecuted by people called Christians. So much persecution and prejudice have prevailed through the centuries that it has produced a complex in the thinking of the Jewish people.

The communal character of their society is more binding than the religious. Many could easily be won to Christ in Jordan and Israel and many other places outside Jordan and Israel, were it not for the community idea. They are part of a family, but they are also a very definite part of the community. To depart from any custom, including the religious, would divorce them from the family and community. Thus, they lose their family and livelihood. If the entire family is converted, that relieves some pressure, but there still remains the community problem. The convert to Christianity is cast out of his society. He loses his job, and is sharply discriminated against in business. He is often scoffed at by all the others. Apart from being a part of the community, he would have no standing. However, it is fair to say that the communal problem is not so real in America, but the family problem still remains. Generally, one is ostracized by his family if he becomes a Christian.

How to Deal with the Jewish People

A correct attitude is imperative. Look at the Jew in the light of his needs and not in the light of his prejudices. He is a sinner. He is guilty before God and is as blind to his condition as the lost Gentile. He is no worse off than the lost Gentile. He is no more or no less guilty of the death of Christ than the Gentile. In dealing with the Jews, do not make a major issue of Jewish guilt in the death of Christ. Of course, we know that they were indeed guilty; but they are no more guilty, as I have already stated, than the Gentiles. The Jew is a human being, lost in his sins. He needs the Saviour.

In approaching the Jewish people:

1. Visit them in their homes. A friendly visit never offends them. The majority of them will appreciate a short visit. They do not resent being invited to religious services.

2. Write friendly letters to them, inviting them to church and especially to special services like revivals.

3. After considerable cultivation, and after his confidence has been established in you, then you may tell him about the Saviour.

4. Follow up with many visits and much instruction. Do not rush the Jew. Give him time to think through all you have said to him. His background is very different from that of the Gentile, and he must be treated thus.

In considering what to say to the Jewish people:

1. Present Christ as the Messiah and Saviour. Some of the Jews do not believe the Old Testament prophecies relative to the Messiah, and those who do believe them have never recognized Christ as the promised Messiah. Regardless of the category in which your prospect may be, he must be led to see Christ as the Saviour, or he can never be won. Point up from the prophecies several definite things about the promised Messiah, and then show from the New Testament how Christ fulfils these detailed prophecies. Point out who the Messiah was, where he came from, how he was to come to earth, and what was to happen to him on earth.

The prophets were clear as to who the Messiah would be. Early in the book of Genesis God predicts the coming of the Messiah to crush the evil of Satan. "And I will put enmity between thee and the woman, and between thy seed and her seed;

it shall bruise thy head, and thou shalt bruise his heel" (Gen. 3:15). This referred to the Messiah in the Targum Pseudo-Jonathan.[6] One may see easily from the Targum that the rabbinic authorities believed in the coming of the Messiah.

As early as nineteen hundred years before Christ the prophet designated the race from which the Messiah would come. God told Abraham, "And in thy seed shall all the nations of the earth be blessed" (Gen. 22:18). The Messiah was to come through the seed of Abraham and was thus to be of the Semitic race. The New Testament establishes that Jesus was of the seed of Abraham (Matt. 1:1–17).

The prophets designated the tribe within the race. "The sceptre shall not depart from Judah, nor a lawgiver from between his feet, until Shiloh come; and unto him shall the gathering of the people be" (Gen. 49:10). Jewish rabbinical authority ascribed this prophecy to the Messiah in Targum Onkelos and Targum Pseudo-Jonathan. The Messiah would come from the tribe of Judah. Two things so far are clear: He was to be of the Semitic race and of the tribe of Judah.

The prophets foretold what family the Messiah would come through. Six hundred years before Christ God said, "Behold, the days come, saith the Lord, that I will raise unto David a righteous Branch, and a King shall reign and prosper, and shall execute judgment and justice in the earth" (Jer. 23:5). The Targum paraphrased this passage to read, "And I will raise up for David the Messiah, the just." The Messiah was to come through the Semitic race, the tribe of Judah, and the family of David. "And Jesse begat David the king" (Matt. 1:6). This statement came from the "book of the generation of Jesus Christ, the son of David, the son of Abraham" (Matt. 1:1).

The prophets even revealed from what town and area the Messiah would come. "But thou, Bethlehem Ephratah, though thou be little among the thousands of Judah, yet out of thee shall he come forth unto me that is to be ruler in Israel; whose goings forth have been from of old, from everlasting" (Mic.

5:2). The town was to be Bethlehem. But there are many Bethlehems, and God made unmistakably clear which town by saying, "Bethlehem Ephratah . . . of Judah."

Many could not understand how the Messiah could be called out of Egypt and at the same time come from Bethlehem. The prophet Hosea had said, "When Israel was a child, then I loved him, and called my son out of Egypt" (11:1). When prophecy had time to become history, it was clear. When Jesus was born in Bethlehem (Luke 2), Herod passed a decree to put all the male children to death from two years old and under (Matt. 2:16). When Herod died, Joseph, the foster father, brought Jesus up to Nazareth from Egypt that "it might be fulfilled which was spoken of the Lord by the prophet, saying, Out of Egypt have I called my son" (Matt. 2:15).

The prophets were clear about how he would come to earth.

He was to be born of a virgin. "Therefore the Lord himself shall give you a sign; Behold, a virgin shall conceive, and bear a son, and shall call his name Immanuel" (Isa. 7:14). This was a strange sign. Only God would choose such a sign. He could have sent the Messiah to the earth in a spectacular fashion. He could have sent him in a chariot of gold drawn by angels, but he chose a method which challenged faith. He chose a method not likely to be imitated by the false Christs.

Gifts were to be presented to the Messiah at his birth (Psalm 72:10). The wise men presented gifts to Jesus in Bethlehem at his birth (Matt. 2:11).

He was to be rejected (Isa. 53:5). He was rejected by his own (John 1:11).

He was to be betrayed by his followers (Psalm 41:9). He was betrayed by Judas (John 13:21).

He was to be sold for thirty pieces of silver. "So they weighed for my price thirty pieces of silver" (Zech. 11:12). "Then one of the twelve, called Judas Iscariot, . . . said unto them, What will ye give me, and I will deliver him unto you? And they covenanted with him for thirty pieces of silver" (Matt. 26:14–

15). The prophet Zechariah uttered this statement hundreds of years before it became history; yet he was very accurate. The prophet even told what would be done with the betrayal money. "And I took the thirty pieces of silver, and cast them to the potter in the house of the Lord" (Zech. 11:13). The New Testament reveals the fulfilment hundreds of years later (Matt. 27:3–7).

The prophets detailed the manner of the death of the Messiah. The prophet declared that he would be crucified. " . . . and they shall look upon me whom they have pierced" (Zech. 12:10). This passage is applied to the Messiah, the son of Joseph, in the Talmud (Sukk. 52a).⁷ "Pierced" refers to the mode of death. It means to be crucified. The Psalms corroborated this statement. "They pierced my hands and my feet" (Psalm 22:16). Zechariah was careful to give the picture in further detail. "And one shall say unto him, What are these wounds in thine hands? Then he shall answer, Those with which I was wounded in the house of my friends" (Zech. 13:6). Death by crucifixion was prophesied for the Messiah here in this Scripture verse two hundred years before the Romans introduced crucifixion to the Hebrews as a mode of capital punishment. This is remarkable and should provoke serious thought.

The prophets tell the reason for the death of the Messiah. "In that day there shall be a fountain opened to the house of David and to the inhabitants of Jerusalem for sin and for uncleanness" (Zech. 13:1). This prophecy declares that the work of the Messiah was not strictly political. He was to atone for sin and to sanctify the people. His work was spiritual. This is the work to which the rabbinical rulers were totally blind, even though it was plainly portrayed in their sacred writings. Isaiah had taught this more than two hundred years before Zechariah. He said, "Yet it pleased the Lord to bruise him; he hath put him to grief: when thou shalt make his soul an offering for sin, he shall see his seed, he shall prolong his days, and the pleasure of the Lord shall prosper in his hand" (Isa. 53:10). The entire twenty-seventh chapter of Matthew is given to revealing when and how the fountain was opened to the house of David. It was opened on the cross at Calvary.

He was to be killed and resurrected. "For thou wilt not leave my soul in hell; neither wilt thou suffer thine Holy One to see corruption" (Psalm 16:10). Peter used this text in the second chapter of Acts to prove that the Messiah would be resurrected from the dead. He states that David did not refer to himself, for his sepulcher is with us now. Peter said, "Therefore being a prophet . . . spake of the resurrection of Christ, that his soul was not left in hell, neither his flesh did see corruption" (Acts 2:30–31).

2. Face frankly the teachings of Isaiah 53. The majority of orthodox Jews will say that the fifty-third chapter of Isaiah does not refer to the Messiah, but rather refers to Israel as a suffering people.

Some will claim that the language of Isaiah 53 is too difficult. The truth is that it is no more difficult than any other prophetic language. It is similar to the language of the prophets in every respect. It is difficult only to those who would try to explain away its clear implications. It is the same as the language of Isaiah 52, and rabbinical authority readily accepts Isaiah 52 as referring to the Messiah.

It does not refer to the Jewish nation, because the one pictured as suffering in Isaiah 53, verses 4, 5, and 8, is suffering for sins of others and not his own.

A review of old rabbinical sources will show that this chapter and other passages used by Christians have also been messianically interpreted by rabbinical authorities. Rabbinical Judaism applied 456 passages in the Old Testament to the Messiah and messianic times. Among these passages is Isaiah 52:13, which reads, "Behold, my servant shall deal prudently, he shall be exalted and extolled, and be very high." The Targum-Jonathan, which is a source of rabbinical authority and was written in the first century A.D., translates it, "Behold, my servant, the Messiah, shall prosper; he shall be high and increase and be exceedingly strong." Here the servant is recognized as a man and not the nation. He is recognized as the Messiah.

In the Yalkut, Volume 2, paragraph 338, the person spoken of in verse 13 is placed above Abraham, Moses, and the angels.[8] The glories and sufferings in this chapter are ascribed to the same person. The Targum does not recognize this, for it ascribes only the glories to the Messiah. This view is untenable and inconsistent. It is inconsistent because in other passages which rabbinical authority recognizes as messianic, the Messiah is pictured as the suffering one. "And I will pour upon the house of David, and upon the inhabitants of Jerusalem, the spirit of grace and of supplications: and they shall look upon me whom they have pierced, and they shall mourn for him, as one mourneth for his only son" (Zech. 12:10). It was not a nation suffering for its own sins or the sins of other nations. It was a Person suffering for the sins of the nation.

In a discussion of 1 Samuel 16:1, the Midrash presents three measures of suffering, and one of them falls to the Messiah.[9] The point of great significance here is that the servant referred to in Isaiah 52:13 and in chapter 53 are one and the same. When rabbinical authority recognized him as the Messiah in chapter 52, verse 13, it undermined the position held by many of them that the word "servant" in chapter 53 refers only to the nation of Israel.

Several great men of rabbinical authority have interpreted Isaiah 53 as referring to the Messiah and not to the suffering nation. Maimonides, who is probably the greatest Talmudic authority of the Middle Ages, held the view that the suffering servant in the fifty-third chapter of Isaiah referred to the Messiah and not to the nation.[10] R. Moshe Cohen Ibn Crispin of Cordova, who also lived in the Middle Ages, states that the fifty-third chapter of Isaiah was given "of God as a description of the Messiah." He goes on to show it was further given to safeguard the people from false Messiahs. A false Messiah would not undergo such sufferings.

Arbabenel, a great rabbinical authority, refused to ascribe the suffering servant idea to the Messiah, but openly admitted that the majority of ancient Jewish authorities understood the passage to refer to the Messiah.[11]

3. Show the Jew his need of the Saviour.

He is a sinner, just as the Gentile. Use Old Testament Scriptures to prove this fact to him. Choice passages for this purpose are: Isaiah 1:18; Isaiah 53:5; Jeremiah 2:13,22; and many others.

Show him that he is in need of the Saviour because Judaism has defaulted in three vital relations.

The first is his relation to the law. If the Jews failed to keep the whole law, they were under a curse. "Cursed be he that confirmeth not all the words of this law to do them" (Deut. 27:26). The Jews were unable to keep the law. Because of their inability to keep the law, God prescribed certain sacrifices symbolically to atone for their failures. These sacrifices were only symbols of the one great sacrifice which was to be made at the coming of the Messiah. These blood sacrifices were to be forever (Lev. 16:34).

The Jews have set aside the entire system of sacrifice today. Why have they set it aside? For one reason, they have no temple. The sacrifice was to be offered only in the Temple (Lev. 17:4,9). Jesus, whom they rejected as Messiah, said that the Temple would be destroyed (Matt. 24:2). This prophecy was fulfilled in A.D. 70. The Temple area is now in the hands of the Arabs and has been in enemy hands most of the time since the death of Christ.

The "as if" solution is not permanent, and has not solved the problem. The "as if" solution held that theocracy no longer existed after the destruction of the Temple, but its constitution remained in force as if it did. The Temple no longer existed, but the Jews in Diaspora bowed and prayed in the direction of the Temple as if it did. The high priest no longer offered blood sacrifices on the Day of Atonement, but the formula was recited on the Day of Atonement as if it did exist. Other practices supplanted the actual sacrifice. Judaism thus became abstract in form. This reconstruction was not to be permanent.

Why have the Jews been forced to adhere to the temporary and abstract system so long? Is not God still alive? Could it not be that the history of the Jews snapped when they rejected Christ? Jewish history is replete with the judgments of God on her when she sinned. Each time when she returned to God, he heard and healed. She has been in one crisis after another with no real proof of the blessings of God since the rejection of Christ before the destruction of the Second Commonwealth.

The Jews have a Day of Atonement, but no atonement.[12] The rabbis instruct the people that the Day of Atonement itself makes atonement. This teaching is contrary to the teaching of their own sacred literature. The day in itself cannot atone. "For on that day shall the priest make an atonement for you" (Lev. 16:30). The Jews have now no authorized priesthood. The Jews have been forced to turn completely from the system ordained of God, because God has permitted the removal both of the Temple and the authorized priesthood. Furthermore, the Old Testament taught that it is the blood that makes an atonement for the soul. "For the life of the flesh is in the blood: and I have given it to you upon the altar to make an atonement for your souls: for it is the blood that maketh an atonement for the soul" (Lev. 17:11).

The soul-winner may ask the Jew pointedly and tenderly why the Temple, the priesthood, and the blood sacrifice have been removed. This may help open his eyes. Point out that their sacred Scriptures teach that a man, the Messiah, would make such an atonement for Israel (Isa. 53:10; Psalm 22:16). The soul-winner may further ask him if it is not remarkably strange that since Jesus was crucified they have lost the Temple, the priesthood, and the blood sacrifice. Remind him that this is a clue. One who is interested in the truth should be willing to follow a sound clue. Show him that this was God's way of replacing the old covenant with the new. Read to him from his Bible the prophecy about the coming of a new covenant (Jer. 31:31–34; Heb. 8:6–9).

His relation to purgatory is another area of failure. Ask him if he knows why the rabbis have created a purgatory which is not mentioned in the law. If he is a well-informed Jew, he will know and admit that such is the case. The writer stood on Mount Moriah in the southwestern section of Jerusalem in a small room adjacent to what is described as the upper room and saw an elderly rabbi say a brief ceremony and burn a candle for the dead loved ones of a group of Jews who were visiting the shrine. Dr. Leroy Gager says, "The invention of a purgatory is a confession of . . . the inability of the old covenant to meet the needs of the soul." [13] The law can only instruct, convict, and lead one to the Saviour. It does not save. "For Christ is the end of the law for righteousness to every one that believeth" (Rom. 10:4). "For we have not an high priest which cannot be touched with the feeling of our infirmities; but was in all points tempted like as we are, yet without sin. Let us therefore come boldly unto the throne of grace, that we may obtain mercy, and find grace to help in time of need" (Heb. 4:15–16).

4. Show him that becoming a Christian does not make him any less a Jew.[14] Point up to him that he becomes a better Jew, because he is then properly related to the Messiah and the nation. Show him that Paul was a fine Jew and was very loyal to his nation after he became a Christian (Rom. 9:1–5). Help him see that national solidarity is impossible apart from God. Help him see that Christ was God's effort to redeem his people.

5. Help him with the persecution problem. Through their family and communal system, they sorely persecute any one of their number who embraces Christianity or any other religion. The fear of being ostracized by his people is the greatest fear

known to the Jew. Since the family and communal ties generally take precedence over religious ties, it poses a great handicap to the converted Jew. No doubt, many Jewish people have recognized Christ as the Messiah but have been afraid to embrace him as Saviour for fear of persecution from their own people.

The soul-winner must console the newly converted Jew with the promises of God. "Blessed are they which are persecuted for righteousness' sake: for theirs is the kingdom of heaven" (Matt. 5:10). Show him that his gain in becoming a real child of God far surpasses any handicaps which may be heaped upon him as a result of his soul's salvation. Point out that the prophets were so persecuted (Matt. 5:12) but that they were blessed of God and live forever. Show him that the real Christian will be happy in spite of any persecution. "And when they had called the apostles, and beaten them, they commanded that they should not speak in the name of Jesus, and let them go. And they departed from the presence of the council, rejoicing that they were counted worthy to suffer shame for his name" (Acts 5:40–41).

Chapter 9

How to Win the Catholics

The Catholic church is a legalistic body. They are a heterogeneous group, bound together by a rigid system of legalism. Roman Catholicism is not something one believes but something one accepts. The majority of Catholics know very little about their beliefs, but they accept certain practices handed down to them by the hierarchy. These people are sincere and hungry hearted. They have a longing in their hearts for something which they do not have. If one can tell them what it is and show them from the Bible how to find it, they can be won.

A Warning for the Soul-Winner

Do not condemn the Catholic Church. Although the Catholic Church has been guilty of scarlet sins, do not use this approach. If the pope, the priest, and the Catholic Church are criticized, the Catholic individual will immediately resent it. He may be aware in some measure of the truth in what you are saying, but he will mistrust you for it.

Never misrepresent the teachings of the Catholic Church. Very few Protestants have a clear conception of what Catholics teach. Fuzzy understanding and unguarded statements are responsible for ineffective personal witness to the Catholics. If one does not understand them and love them, he will never win

116

them. A misrepresentation, whether done in ignorance or wilfully, is disastrous. If one would learn what Catholics believe, let him read what they claim for themselves and not what their enemies say about them. A consecrated soul-winner will be fair. He will never stoop to unfair tactics. No one need misrepresent the Catholics, for they have enough errors without being misrepresented. Refrain from the use of anti-Catholic literature. This will defeat your purpose. You must win his respect and good will before you can win his soul to Christ.

Do not try to get a decision too soon. Often your clear explanations of the Word of God will anger him. If they do, do not persist. Leave it for the time, and come back to the point again in due season. Take him each time as far as you can without "letting the fish off the hook." Win a Catholic just as you would catch a fish. It is a give-and-take proposition. Let him have the line; then draw him a little more closely until he is safely in the boat.

Elementary Things Which the Soul-Winner Must Know

Catholics are making great inroads in America and everywhere. They are involved in every phase of national and community life. Great numbers of news analysts are Catholics. They have captured strategic posts of opportunity in our nation. They are strong in almost all of our great American cities. They are predominant in South America, the Philippine Islands, Europe, and many places in the world. They are aggressive. One is not dealing with an archaic element of Christianity when he comes to grips with Catholicism. He is dealing with a Christian perversion, and a subtle and aggressive one.

Contact individuals rather than masses. It is difficult to contact them in masses. The local priest will, in most cases, prevent this. It is better to cultivate them individually and in piecemeal teach them the true plan of salvation.

Be friendly and kind. All people admire the friendly touch. Even animals will respond to kindness. Genuine kindness will unarm almost anyone. When people respect the soul-winner, they will let him close enough to them to preach Christ. This is also true of Catholics.

Use the Roman Catholic Bible. This is the Douay Version. They have been taught that the Protestant Bible is corrupt. It is, therefore, better to use the Catholic Bible. It is the same as the Protestant Bible except for a few translations and the misleading footnotes on each page. The text is there. Read it, and let the Holy Spirit use it to convict of sin.

The Nature of Roman Catholic Salvation

It is imperative that the soul-winner understand the nature of the Catholic view of salvation. If he is conversant with it, he will know where to begin. He will know what to say to unhinge his prospect and to lead him to personal faith in Christ.

Catholic salvation is uncertain.[1] The Catholic has no assurance of salvation. He does not know whether he is saved or not. His is only a hope, because he must go through purgatory before he can be sure of his salvation. The Catholic teachers claim that one is cleansed through the fires of purgatory.[2] Purgatory is part of the Catholic's plan of salvation. Since it is part of the plan of salvation, no one is sure of salvation until he has passed through the fires of purgatory. Thus, their salvation is uncertain, because certain temporal penalties for venial sins may fall on one in purgatory.[3]

It is intermediated. Individuals have no direct access to God. Catholics teach that Christ gave power to forgive sins to his apostles and their successors. This teaching is found in *The Catechism Explained* by Spirago and Clarke.[4] They further state that he who would have his sins forgiven must go to the bishop or the priest. The intermediaries are the Church, the priest, the Virgin Mary, and the saints.

The Catholic salvation is sacramental. Salvation is obtained by observing the sacraments. It is strictly mechanical. The Catholics say that sacraments are sensible signs instituted by

Christ, by means of which the grace of the Holy Spirit is communicated to us.[5] In addition to the signs instituted by Christ, certain ceremonies have been instituted by the church to indicate still more perceptibly that grace is conferred. These ceremonies increase the devotions of those who receive the sacraments.

There are seven sacraments, and five of them are essential to salvation. Those which are essential to salvation are baptism, confirmation, Eucharist, penance, and extreme unction.

Baptism.—Through baptism the person is cleansed from original sin and every sin. According to the Catholics, there are two kinds of sins, namely, mortal and venial. There are seven great sins which they designate as mortal, and all others are venial. Baptism remits both mortal and venial sins. It also cleanses from the guilt and punishment of sins. Catholics claim that one not only receives remission for all kinds of sin at baptism, but is gifted with habitual and sanctifying grace and becomes a child of God, an heir of heaven, and also a member of the Church.

Baptism is so indispensably necessary to salvation that a child who dies unbaptized cannot enter heaven.[6] They claim that the reason for such belief is that every child coming into the world has the taint of original sin and has no sanctifying grace, without which no man can enter heaven. This does not mean that the child goes to hell, because he has not committed actual sin.

Baptism is so indispensably necessary to salvation that Catholics permit anyone, even heretics and Jews, to perform baptism in case of an emergency, provided it is correctly administered—that is, if the water is poured on the head or any part of the body while the correct formula is repeated. If baptism of water is impossible, then the baptism of desire may be substituted. In *The Catechism Explained* they say that formerly baptism was by immersion, but sometimes water was poured on, or even sprinkled on, the person.[7]

The sacrament of confirmation.—Confirmation is to strengthen the faith of the Catholic. They claim that the Holy Spirit is received at baptism, but not in all of his fulness. Therefore, the Holy Spirit is received in his fulness at confirmation. Confirmation is to the Catholic what the day of Pentecost was to the early Christian.

The bishop makes the sign of the cross on the person's brow, pours oil upon the head, strikes the person on the cheek, and lays his hand upon him. Those who are confirmed are to receive the gift of the Holy Ghost during the ceremony.

The supernatural effect of the ceremony is to create a spirit of meekness and increase charity toward God and the neighbors. It is supposed to enlighten one's understanding, strengthen his will, and preserve his soul.

The Eucharist.—Through the Eucharist one eats the consecrated bread and thereby receives Christ. The bread and wine actually become the body and blood of Christ. Through the Eucharist one receives the divinity, the body and blood of Christ.[8] This sacrament is designated as the "holy sacrament of the altar." The purpose of this sacrament is to attain spiritual perfection here and life hereafter. The catechism plainly states that Holy Communion is essential to the final attainment of eternal salvation.[9] The Eucharist remits the guilt of venial sins, but not the penalty.

The sacrament of penance.—Penance and confession go together. The act of penance is a good deed, a pilgrimage, a denial to self of something, or a buffeting of the body done to remit sins. The person will kneel in the confessional, make the sign of the cross, and receive the priest's blessing. He then recites the first part of the confiteor. Then the priest asks him questions, sets him a penance, gives absolution, and dismisses him. The individual then in due time does his penance. Penance remits all mortal sins committed since his baptism. Without penance a person cannot recover the justice he has lost (Council of Trent 14, 1; 6, 29). It may be well to remember that the priest does not pray for absolution, but he bestows it. This statement can be verified by any book on Catholic catechism.

Extreme unction.—In extreme unction, the priest anoints the sick or dying with consecrated oil upon the organs of his five senses and prays over him. He anoints with oil in the form of the cross upon the eyes, nose, mouth, ears, hands, and feet, and at every unction repeats the following prayer: "Through this holy unction and through His most tender mercy, may the Lord pardon thee whatsoever sins thou hast committed by seeing, hearing," etc. They claim that extreme unction acts spiritually as does oil materially. It strengthens, heals, and assists the soul to attain eternal salvation. Extreme unction compensates for all that the sick man left incomplete in the sacrament of penance. They claim that extreme unction often heals the sick physically as well as spiritually. Extreme unction, however, can only be administered to those in danger of death. Before this sacrament is administered, the sick is supposed to confess his sins and receive Holy Communion.

Their doctrine of purgatory adds more confusion to the uncertainty of salvation. All must pass through purgatory. Purgatory is the state or place where the souls of the faithful go after death. The stay in purgatory is shortened by indulgences and suffrages. While one is alive, he may make donations to worthy causes, visit shrines, make pilgrimages, and do other prescribed things to gain merit. This remits certain temporal punishments and is called "indulgences." These indulgences will shorten one's stay in purgatory. Suffrages are indulgences secured for a deceased loved one to shorten his stay in purgatory. No one knows, however, how long a person remains in purgatory.

How to Deal with Catholics

Tell him that he can be assured of salvation. Make plain that salvation is not merely a future hope but a present reality. If the soul-winner is familiar with the nature of Catholic salvation, he will know that they have no certainty of salvation. Let the soul-winner ask him if he is sure of his salvation. He will reply that he is not and cannot be assured. He does not know in this life if he has earned enough merits to go directly into the acceptance of God. He has been taught that he cannot know until he dies. Then tell him that his Bible teaches that he can and should know if he has the right relationship with God and if he has true salvation. Seek to create a doubt in his mind. Then prove your position with the Bible. Point up to him what the Bible says on the subject.

Read John 5:24 and explain it. It says, "Verily, verily, I say unto you, He that heareth my word, and believeth on him that sent me, hath everlasting life, and shall not come into condemnation; but is passed from death unto life." Show him that it plainly says "hath everlasting life." Tell him that this expression means now. It does not refer to the future.

Then read slowly and patiently explain 1 John 5:13. "These things have I written unto you that believe on the name of the Son of God; that ye may know that ye have eternal life, and that ye may believe on the name of the Son of God." Tell him that this statement refers to the book of 1 John and that God has made it possible for all true believers to know that they have "eternal life." If one does not have the assurance of eternal life here and now, it is because he has not read the book of 1 John or does not have eternal life. Show him that if he has no assurance and can have none, he has the type of salvation which is foreign to the salvation that God gives and teaches about in the New Testament. If this disturbs him, then proceed to preach salvation through a personal experience with Christ.

You may also help the Catholic with Romans 8:14. "For as many as are led by the Spirit of God, they are the sons of God." Explain to him that if anyone is led by the Spirit of God, he is a son of God. He not only will finally be a son of God at the end of the way, but is, according to this verse, a son of God now. Ask him, "If you are not now a son of God and won't be until after purgatory, is not your position in direct conflict with

God's plan of salvation and God's way for true Christians?" Show him that true Christians are sons of God now as they are led by the Spirit of God.

Teach the Catholic that salvation is spiritual and not sacramental. He has been taught that salvation is sacramental and mechanical. Use the following Scriptures:

"For by grace are ye saved through faith; and that not of yourselves: it is the gift of God: not of works, lest any man should boast" (Eph. 2:8-9). This plain Scripture passage proves that the salvation of Jesus Christ is not by "works," that is, by ceremonies of the church or deeds of the individual. Salvation is spiritual. Salvation is by the "grace" of God. In this verse the spiritual is set over against the ceremonial. Spiritual salvation is totally of God, and ceremonial salvation depends on man. He may reply that this makes salvation too easy and will lead to immoral and careless living. This reveals that he does not yet understand the nature of spiritual salvation. Show him that when one becomes a child of God by a transforming experience with God his nature is changed and he will hate sin and will desire to do right. Here one may use John 3:1-5.

John 3:1-5 declares the nature of spiritual salvation. One is born again and thus becomes a new creation in Christ. Stay with this passage. If you leave it, do so only temporarily. Build the most of your discussion around this great Scripture passage. Almost any Catholic who can be won at all can be won with this particular Scripture.

"For God so loved the world, that he gave his only begotten Son, that whosoever believeth in him should not perish, but have everlasting life" (John 3:16). Dr. Eugene Harrison presents a unique way to use this verse.[10] He suggests that the soul-winner read the verse slowly, as he runs a pencil under the words, and make it read, "For God so loved the world, that he gave his only begotten Son, that whosoever believeth in him—and faithfully observes confessions, masses, penance, and seasons of self-denial, and says 'Hail Mary' frequently, and supplicates the saints—should not perish, but have everlasting life." The Catholic will almost always say, "But I do not see those things there." Then the winner of souls may say: "You are correct. They are not there. And neither are they to be found anywhere in all your Bible." This may be an unhinging revelation to the prospect.

Point up to him that Christ is our only mediator. He has been taught that salvation is intermediated, that one receives salvation through Mary, the saints, the Church, and the priest.

"For there is one God, and one mediator between God and men, the man Christ Jesus" (1 Tim. 2:5). One must deal gently with the veneration of Mary. Catholics are more easily inflamed about Mary than about purgatory. The doctrine about Mary is very precious to them. In theory, they adore Mary rather than worship her. They claim to venerate Mary but not to worship her as they do God. The language of their veneration seems to be the same as that of worship, however. We must meet this fallacy gently with the Bible. Read and explain the words of Christ: "I am the way, the truth, and the life: no man cometh unto the Father, but by me" (John 14:6). Point up that Jesus is the way to God, and the only way. Make it clear that Jesus said he was the way. He loved his mother, but in none of his statements did he declare that she was the way to God. She said very few recorded words. She did say, "Whatsoever he saith unto you, do it" (John 2:5). Jesus said, "Come unto me, all ye that labour and are heavy laden, and I will give you rest" (Matt. 11:28). He claimed for himself, "I am the door: by me if any man enter in, he shall be saved" (John 10:9). These Scriptures thoroughly explained and gently applied will help.

Pray with the Catholic. Never enter the home of anyone without praying before you depart. Ask the Catholic if you may pray for him. Very few will refuse. Most of them will welcome it, and many will even offer to pay you for it at the close of the prayer. You will explain that you are happy to pray for him and with him and that there are no charges. To help him see that he must pray for himself to God, read and explain Romans 10:13. Show him the difference between reading prayers and talking directly to God out of the heart. The disciples of John were taught to make prayers (Luke 5:33). Jesus prayed in the presence of his disciples (Luke 9:18) and later taught them to pray (Luke 11:1–4). When the Catholic hears a child of God pray directly and warmly to God, he is drawn nearer to God, and often longs to have such access to the heart of God.

Urge the Catholic to read the Bible. If he does not have a copy, give him one.

Show him that it is permissible by the Catholic Church for him to read the Catholic version of the Bible. The Douay Version is called the "Confraternity Edition." Pope Benedict XV has a note in the edition, urging them to read the Bible, and they are given indulgences of three hundred days for every fifteen minutes that they read from the Bible.[11] It is good to point this out to them because some of them may not know it. For the present, you will say nothing of indulgences, but will get him to read the Bible. The Bible is a profitable book for anyone who does not know Christ as his Saviour and who believes that he is saved by good deeds or ceremonies. The Bible produces saving faith. "So then faith cometh by hearing, and hearing by the word of God" (Rom. 10:17).

Direct him in reading the Bible. Let him contrast certain Scriptures on the plan of salvation in the Confraternity version and the Protestant version. This will help him see that there is virtually no difference in the two versions and will help him see that he has been unduly guarded by his leaders. It will remove some of his mistrust. It will teach him the difference between salvation by sacraments and spiritual salvation. Assign certain great passages to him to study, and then come back and go over those passages with him, giving him an explanation of their meaning. It may be well to assign such passages as John 3:1–16 for his study. Try to answer any questions which may arise in his mind. Do not press him too soon for a decision. Exercise great patience and common sense. At the proper time, urge him to accept Christ as Saviour. You will not need to urge him to join the church. When he comes to know Christ as personal Saviour, he will soon see that there is a difference between the church that preached the true plan of salvation to him and one that failed. In due time, you can properly guide him into the church that will feed his soul and strengthen his life.

Chapter 10

How to Win the Spiritists

There are large numbers of people who are not of our religious and cultural background who need the Saviour. The fact that they live in an atmosphere foreign to our cultural surroundings and that there is definitely present a psychological hindrance does not excuse us from our obligation to win them to Christ. Lack of compatibility between people of various groups is no real reason to steer clear of them evangelistically. Some victims of the cults were once nominal Baptists, Methodists, or of some other group, but the most of them are from a background vastly different from the average evangelical. A knowledge of this fact is essential in dealing with them, but should in no case divert one from dealing frankly and immediately with them. Anyone who does not believe that Jesus Christ is the Son of God and who has never accepted Christ as his Saviour should be a challenge to the soul-winner.

The purpose of Satan is to confuse the people. If he can lead people into half-truths and into religious error and darken their minds, he has succeeded in his mission. If he can occupy their lives and dissipate their energy in a spurious religion which satisfies their innate hunger for God, he has gloriously succeeded. His purpose is to drive a wedge between God and men. It does not matter how it is accomplished. He would as soon lose a man in religious confusion as to drown him in alcohol or imprison him in immorality. One of his greatest triumphs in the twentieth century is in the realm of the cults.

We shall deal briefly with the spiritists, because this is the oldest of all the cults, and it is spreading with appalling rapidity in the great cities of America and the world. We shall briefly set forth their origin and what they believe and offer a few suggestions as to how to deal with them.

Origin of the Spiritists

The psychological reason for the spiritists is based on the loneliness which possesses folk who have lost loved ones in death. Death enters abruptly and takes away a loved one and leaves an aching void. The bereaved are sad and lonely. They want assurance that death does not end it all. People are haunted with the questions: Do we live again? Are our dead loved ones conscious of us? Shall we see them again? Will they know us? What shall we do now while we wait? In hours of great sorrow people are very gullible. They are like a drowning man grasping at a straw. Just at this point the devil enters to lead the weary astray. He promises them through spiritism that the dead are conscious of them and long to contact them. He tells the sorrowing that one does not need to wait until death to communicate with their precious ones. He tells them that they can here and now communicate with the dead. Spiritists offer an extravagant system of communication. Much of what is done is pure fakery, but much of it is demon activity, and to sit in the presence of its performance is more dangerous than sitting on an atomic bomb while it is being detonated.

Spiritism is a term applied to the belief in the actuality of intercourse between the living and the dead. This belief has been held for many centuries. It is the oldest religious delusion in history. It has existed in almost all stages of culture. Traces of spiritism were found among the ancient Egyptians, Babylonians, and Hindus.[1] In the Roman Empire manifestations similar to those common to spiritism were reported. Spiritism was prevalent in Bible times, and the Bible is plain in denouncing it. Since the middle of the nineteenth century, spiritism has made great inroads in the United States.[2] The movement in America goes back to the "Rochester knockings." These knockings were first heard in the home of John D. Fox of Hydeville, New York. His two daughters, Margaret and Kate, were sensitive to it and claimed to contact the spirits. After the family moved to nearby Rochester, the knockings continued. The phenomena grew in intensity all over the entire area. The phenomena consisted of table rappings, playing on musical instruments, spirit writing, and appearance of objects in the atmosphere.

No attempt was made to organize a national association until 1863. In 1852 the movement had already spread to England and had gathered great momentum there. By 1945 there were reported 228,000 adherents to the movement in the U.S.A.[3] A revival of spiritism came with each of the two world wars. When people are grieved by the loss of loved ones, this cult thrives.

What the Spiritists Believe

They believe that God is pantheistic. He is not a person. He is a principle, or a moving force. Their conception of God is also polytheistic. They say that there are as many gods as there are types of persons and minds needing a god. God is the presence of the infinite spirit or principle acting by the law of mediation.[4]

As to the person and work of Christ, they believe that Christ is not uniquely divine. "He is divine in the sense that all men are potentially divine."[5] The miraculous conception of Christ is a fabrication. The name of Christ is not used in their hymnbook.

To the spiritist, Christ was a medium of the high order. He was only a medium, and is today no higher than the sixth heaven. All men may attain this level. Some men are in the seventh heaven. They claim that people on earth are surrounded by several layers of existence called "heavens." They are designated as the first, second, third heaven, etc. Spirits inhabit these realms. They believe it is possible to contact these spirits. People with highly developed "soul force" or who are highly psychic may in one of several ways make contact with disembodied spirits. Those who contact the dead are called mediums.

There are three ways to communicate with the spirits.

Table rappings is one of the most common means of contact. Psychic force is made stronger when several people form physical contact with each other. They sit in a circle around the table and place their hands upon the table, with thumbs and little fingers joined so as to complete the physical contact circle. The sitters agree with the spirit that one tap of the table leg means "A" and two taps mean "B," etc. The message is spelled out through the number of taps.

In the second place, the medium may go into a trance. Bodily consciousness is suspended for a time. The medium reports what she hears or sees while in the trance. Often the sitters may ask questions and the medium will answer. Sometimes the medium will write the message she claims to receive from the spirits. When the medium comes out of the trance, she often does not remember what transpired.

The third method of communication is materialization. The spirit which is being contacted is materialized. Sometimes the materialization is in the form of floating objects, etc.

Then there was the atonement. They believe that the death of Jesus was no more than an unfortunate and untimely affair. The death of Christ does not atone for sin. The doctrine of atonement is to the spiritist a survival of a spiritual abuse and is immoral to the core.[6] They say that there is no justice in a vicarious sacrifice.[7] To the spiritist, Jesus was a reformer in Judea, a medium, and was no more than just that.

Their conception of sin is fatalistic. Man's path, good or bad, is divinely ordered. They make no real distinction between good and evil. Man has no control over his actions. In essence, they deny the fact of sin. They claim that man never fell. They call the story of the fall of man an outrageous lie.[8]

They deny the doctrine of the forgiveness of sins. Man saves himself by his own actions. Of course, they are inconsistent here, because if man has no control over his actions, how could he save himself by his actions? They place great emphasis on right living here on earth, for their status in the spirit world depends on what they do here. Correct living, however, has more to do with their participation in the séance and the propagation of the conceptions of spiritism than with the mode of living. Spirit contact in this world is the main means of advancement for spiritists. The realm to which one goes at death depends on his works here. His works consist largely of sending and receiving spirit messages. All people are subject to a better development of what they call "soul force."

As to life after death, the individual continues to exist after the change called death, and communication with the disembodied spirit is a proven fact. The doorway to change and spiritual advancement does not end at death.[9] Those who have defied the laws of intelligence (spiritism) while on earth will suffer in the hereafter by trying in vain to continue their evil ways. But this confusion called "suffering" caused by thwarted evil desires will not be eternal. It will lead to complete purification, beginning with remorse and passing through spiritual and intellectual reformation.

How to Deal with Spiritists

The purpose of this discussion is to prevent many from falling into this deadly error. It is far easier to prevent this perversion than to reclaim one who has fallen into it. Every pastor would do well to preach a series of sermons every few years on the cults, taking up one at a time and in loving-kindness pointing up their errors and giving the plain, positive Bible teachings which disprove their position. Although this treatment is primarily to prevent, it is also to encourage the soul-winner that these people can be won from the error of their way and brought to Christ the Saviour. Many have been won, and many more will be by the grace of God.

Realize fully the spiritual condition of the spiritist. He is not merely a plain sinner, but he is also the victim of a deadly delusion. Some of them are wilful charlatans, but most of them are sincere. A blind man is not aware of the five-thousand-foot precipice just below him because he cannot see. The cultist is blind spiritually. The devil has deliberately blinded him. Blindness is no sign of obstinacy, but rather it is a condition to be dealt with. These spiritually blind people are honest. They believe they are right. Let the soul-winner exercise patience and great love in dealing with them. "In whom the god of this world hath blinded the minds of them which believe not, lest the light of the glorious gospel of Christ, who is the image of God, should shine unto them" (2 Cor. 4:4).

Give the spiritist your warm testimony and do not try to be a lawyer. You need not argue the case. He is mentally confused, and his mind is satiated with arguments. He will not be convinced, but he may be touched by the Spirit of God. Tell him in the gentle spirit of Jesus what Christ has done for you. Show him how Jesus has helped you in life and how he enables you now. Show him why he should try Christ. Help him to see that an experience with Christ makes a difference.

One cannot win the spiritist with the arguments of the head, but he may be won with the heart. Heart power, and not intellectual power, is the answer in dealing with the spiritist. Let him witness something in your spirit which is from above. The spirit of Christ is contagious.

The spiritist is not a hardheaded legalist. He is satanically influenced. No soul-winner is a match for Satan, but the Holy Spirit is more than sufficient. Throw out the truth to him, but let him decide. Do not try to push him into a decision. Let him make his own judgments. Be careful to present the correct attitude. Never let him get the idea that you are trying to convince him. If you do, he will resist you; he will resent it and will determine that you will not convince him. He will say in his heart: "Well, this upstart thinks he can prove that I am wrong, does he? I am no weakling. He will see."

Recently a soul-winner was dealing with a man and his wife who were victims of a kindred cult, and when they said that they did not believe in the Trinity and other fundamental doctrines, the soul-winner refused to be diverted with related questions. You do not need to answer all related questions to win a soul. The soul-winner would say to this couple: "That is an important question which you have raised, but the most important thing is your relation to Christ. Get that settled first, and it will be less difficult to understand the related problems which you are now facing." He would read unhurriedly the Scriptures on the problems which they had raised, but with no explanation, and then he would proceed to present Christ as the only Saviour. He won the two dear people. He did it with the heart and not with the head. He manifested the spirit of Christ. He did not outargue them. He saw these fine people baptized into the church, and he saw them winning souls within a week's time. Let the soul-winner use the heart more than the head.

Give the spiritist God's Word. Read the Bible to him, and rely on it to do its work. Show him with all tenderness from the Word of God that trafficking with the spirits is unlawful.

The book of the Law teaches that any kind of seeking after the dead is unlawful and forbidden. "There shall not be found among you any one that . . . useth divination, or an observer of times, or an enchanter, or a witch, or a charmer, or a consulter with familiar spirits, . . . for all that do these things are an abomination unto the Lord" (Deut. 18:10–12). Familiar spirits are spirits who are supposed to respond to the medium who has power over them. Van Baalen said they were probably called "familiar" spirits because they were servants subject to the wishes of the owner.[10] This Old Testament Scripture passage declares that such practice is an abomination to the Lord, and must be cut off from among the people.

"Thou shalt not suffer a witch to live" (Ex. 22:18). A witch was, according to the Hebrew word, a woman with the spirit of divination.

"And the soul that turneth after such as have familiar spirits . . . I will even set my face against that soul, and will cut him off from among his people" (Lev. 20:6). It is true that the spiritist leaders are aware that the Bible is against them, and they openly declare that that part of the Bible is untrustworthy which disagrees with them. Do not let this position, however. prevent you from reading these Scriptures to the cultist. Remember that "faith cometh by hearing, and hearing by the word of God" (Rom. 10:17). The Word of God breeds faith. It is the origin of faith. The Word of God, whether believed or not, gives rise to faith that saves. Read the Bible to them, and let the Holy Spirit use it. It is the sword of the Spirit.

The New Testament opposes contact with the spirits. "Now the Spirit speaketh expressly, that in the latter times some shall depart from the faith, giving heed to seducing spirits, and doctrines of devils" (1 Tim. 4:1).

The New Testament declares that anything which denies the humanity of Jesus is of the devil. "Every spirit that confesseth that Jesus Christ is come in the flesh is of God: and every spirit that confesseth not that Jesus Christ is come in the flesh is not of God: and this is that spirit of antichrist, whereof ye have heard that it should come; and even now already is it in the world" (1 John 4:2–3).

The Bible tells us all that we need to know about the life after death and the state of our loved ones out there. Lazarus spent four days out there, but he came back with his finger on his lips. He gave no account of his experiences in the land of the dead (John 11:38–44). Paul was caught up into the third heaven, but he said he had orders to speak not of what he saw because it was unlawful (2 Cor. 12:4). The Bible, however, tells us enough to comfort in sorrow and to kindle the brightest hopes for renewed fellowship with our deceased loved ones in heaven.

Jesus warned against the séance in his illustration of the man who died and in hell lifted up his eyes and saw Abraham in a distant place and sought help from Abraham. He urged Abraham to send Lazarus to his father's house to warn his five brothers about the future state of the lost. Here Jesus condemned the séance. "And he said unto them, If they hear not Moses and the prophets, neither will they be persuaded, though one rose from the dead" (Luke 16:31).

At this point the spiritist may say, "See, they have access to Moses and the prophets." You will be careful to point up that they have Moses and the prophets not through mediums, but in the holy Scriptures. It seems that Jesus anticipated such fallacious thinking when he uttered a death-dealing blow to it as he talked with the disciples on the way to Emmaus. "And beginning at Moses and all the prophets, he expounded unto them in all the scriptures the things concerning himself" (Luke 24:27). He began at Moses and the prophets not with a séance, but by reading and expounding the holy Scriptures.

In all love, show him why God does not permit contact with the spirits.

The spirits of our beloved dead do not want to come back. The whole system of spiritism is built on a fallacious notion that the spirits are lonely and that they wish contact with us. First Samuel 28 is the only place in the whole Bible where it is recorded that a person with a spirit of divination ever brought back the spirit of the dead. There are many doubtful things about that account, but if it is true, it establishes two things for sure, the first being, Samuel did not want to be contacted. "And Samuel said to Saul, Why hast thou disquieted me, to bring me up? . . . Wherefore then dost thou ask of me, seeing the Lord is departed from thee . . . ?" (1 Sam. 28:15–16). It teaches also that God condemns it. "So Saul died for his transgression which he committed against the Lord, even against the word of the Lord, which he kept not, and also for asking counsel of one that had a familiar spirit, to enquire of it; And enquired not of the Lord" (1 Chron. 10:13–14).

Contact with the spirits would lead to ancestor worship. People in sorrow and in trouble would go around God to the spirits of their loved ones. "For it is written, Thou shalt worship the Lord thy God, and him only shalt thou serve" (Matt. 4:10).

Explain to him the simple plan of salvation. If he shows real concern, then use the same Scriptures which you would employ to win the concerned to Christ.

Chapter 11

How to Win the Doubters

The doubter is in reality a skeptic. He must not, however, be confused with the atheist. The atheist does not believe in the existence of God. The doubter does not denounce the existence of God, but merely declares that he doubts certain Bible preachments about God. He is skeptical of the cardinal truths set forth in the Bible about God and Christ. The doubter may have some vague conception of God, but would deny that Christ is the Son of God. If he denies that Jesus is the Son of God, he is to that degree an infidel. The main difficulty with the doubter is in the realm of knowledge as well as heart. His information concerning God is either incomplete or incorrect. Often the doubter operates on a false assumption —that all fields of knowledge can be subjected to rationality.

There are two kinds of doubters. They may be classified as the insincere and the sincere doubter. It is necessary to discover which category a doubter is in before dealing with him. The two types are poles apart, and the approach suited to one would not reach the other. The soul-winner must make sure whether the doubter is insincere or honest.

The Insincere Doubter

The insincere skeptic is not really a doubter. He uses his skeptical arguments to throw up a smoke screen and to hide from the public his real difficulty. His trouble is actually unbelief. He is a deep-dyed sinner, and he knows it, but he labors to make others believe that he doubts God. He thinks that intellectual confusion is more respectable than moral bankruptcy. He is morally rotten. Ordinarily, he is living a double life, and would deliberately justify himself on the grounds that the accepted teachings about God are not trustworthy. He sets himself to the task of casting doubts on the reality of God and that Jesus is the Saviour. This is a hiding place for his insincere skepticism.

How to Deal with the Dishonest Skeptic

Test him to make sure if he is dishonest. A soul-winner spoke to such a man about his soul recently. The person said: "I do not believe that Jesus is the Son of God or the Saviour of the world. I have just finished the university, and while there, I learned too much to accept the childish notions about God." The soul-winner talked for a while with him, then asked him to try God and test the laws of the spiritual world by praying five minutes a day for the next seven days. He said, "Then I shall return, and let us see what you think then of God." The doubter answered, "No, I won't promise to pray five minutes a day for the next seven days, for if I did, I would at the end of the seven days be as you are." He was right; he knew what would happen. His refusal to follow the simple clue revealed to the soul-winner that he was not honest.

Use the shock treatment. Dr. L. R. Scarborough suggests that the shock treatment should often be used to uncover the real reason for the apparent skepticism of the insincere skeptic.[1] The insincere doubter is covering up his real condition, and should be shocked into realizing what he is doing. Let him know that you know what constitutes his real trouble. The fact that you bluntly uncover him may shock him. When you have him off guard, give to him the simple plan of salvation, and urge him to trust Christ as Saviour. An excellent Scripture reference to use for shock purposes is 1 Corinthians 2:14 and 2 Corinthians 4:3–4.

The Honest Doubter

The honest doubter is truly a skeptic. He actually doubts the fundamentals about God and Christ. His doubts are generally due to contact with skeptical writings by some smoky-brained individual. In a few instances, his doubts may stem from the slovenly living of professed Christians. Do not forget, however, that beneath all doubts is sin. He is a sinner. His nature, therefore, is conducive to doubt. In any case, he is a sincere doubter, and should be treated as such.

How to Deal with an Honest Doubter

Discover the source of his doubts if possible. Often the answer to his skepticism will lie in the origin of his doubts. If his doubts stem from reading skeptical literature, then ask him if he has read the preponderance of literature which presents the other side. Point up to him that for every page written casting dispersions on revealed religion, there are thousands of pages written by men just as scholarly, defending and setting forth the validity of the great religious fundamentals.

Ask questions to provoke thought. Help him to see that he believes more of the fundamentals than he claims to believe or even thought he believed. Question him in such a way as to help him see that his unbelief is without foundation.[2] When you have him write down on a sheet of paper the things he does not believe and then write out the reasons for not believing them, it will be a revelation to him. This procedure will provoke thought. This is his great need. He has been thinking the twisted thoughts of others. When he begins to think for himself, the soul-winner is in position to tell him how to believe.

Show him how to believe. "If any man will do his will, he shall know of the doctrine, whether it be of God, or whether I speak of myself" (John 7:17). Explain in detail this Scripture verse. Slice it into small pieces, and feed it to him. It is the bread from heaven for a doubter.

Ask him if he wants to know the will of God. He is an honest skeptic and is actually willing to know. He will answer yes. Explain that he must want to know and do the will of God.

Ask him if he is willing to make an honest effort to find and do God's will. He will again answer yes.

Then ask him if he believes in prayer. He will answer no, for he is honest. If his answer is no, then ask him how he knows that he does not believe in prayer, since he has never tried it. Tell him that if he has never tried it he is not in position to say whether he believes it or not. Show him that prayer is a clue. Everyone who is honestly searching for a truth must be open to follow any clue. Get him to agree to pray to God as he reads the Scriptures, asking God for guidance.

Point up that it is God's will for man to pray. Read here again, "If any man will do his will, he shall know." Use as an illustration the healing of the palsied man recorded in the second chapter of Mark. Jesus said to the palsied man, "Arise, and take up thy bed, and go thy way into thine house. And immediately he arose, took up the bed, . . ." (Mark 2:11–12). When Jesus commanded him to arise and pick up his bed, the palsied man might have replied, "Why, see here, I haven't walked in years," etc. Instead, "he arose, took up the bed, and went forth before them all" (Mark 2:12).

When did healing come to him? When he acted, when he obeyed the command, when he did the will of Christ and got up from the pallet. As he put forth the effort to get up, God gave him the healing. Point out that this is the case of the doubter. When he does the will of God, he will know and receive the benefits of God. To read the Word of God and to pray asking for guidance is an effort in the direction of doing God's will.

Ask him to read prayerfully the Word of God. Guide him in his reading. Select suitable Scriptures. The Gospel of John is the best Scripture reading for the skeptic. Read John 20:31, and explain to him that the entire book was written for the purpose of helping men believe that Jesus is the Christ, the Son of God, and that when one believes in Christ he receives life.

Use the pragmatic approach. Get the skeptic to admit that some realities are not known through the purely rational approach but rather through experience. Help him to see that beauty and love are such realities. Help him to see that experience, and not pure reason, proves the love of his mother. It takes no keen rationalization to become aware of the beauty of the rose or a piece of art. One only needs to come into contact with a flower garden or an art gallery. It will not be difficult to get him to admit that some phases of reality do not require rationality. Use this fact as a basis to try to get him to concede that spiritual religion could be a similar field and could be known by experience.

Then proceed to tell him about your experience with God. Show him how by faith you contacted God and came to the conviction that God is real. You may also give him the experience of others whose background was totally different from yours, and yet they had the same redeeming experience with God through Christ. It would be well to give him the authenticated testimonies of men who once hated Christ and opposed Christianity. Lew Wallace is a classic illustration.

While governor of the territory of New Mexico, Mr. Wallace set out to write a book to disprove Christ and to show him up as a myth. To do so, he had to read the Gospels which recorded the life and activities of Christ. It was also necessary for him to read the prophets that prophesied the coming of the Christ. In his serious study, he met the Nazarene face to face, and was convicted of his sins and converted. Instead of writing a criticism of Jesus, he wrote the great religious novel *Ben-Hur*. Experience is a mighty argument in favor of reality.

Then there is the epistemological approach.[3] Many doubters are skeptical about the existence of God. Some are skeptical about the deity of Christ and one thing or another. But the major difficulty with the average skeptic centers around God and Christ. Ask him, "Have you been everywhere?" He will admit readily that he has not traveled everywhere. It is possible to visit every nation on earth and still not explore every place in the land. Then you may ask, "How do you know that God is not in some of the places you have not visited?" Ask him, "Have you seen everything?" He will answer no. If not in words, he will think it. Then say, "How do you know that God is not in the things you have not seen?" Ask him further, "Do you know everything?" Of course he will recognize that no one does. No one could master one field of knowledge in an entire lifetime, much less claim to know everything. Then say to him, "You do not know everything, and God could be in the great realms of knowledge unknown to you." He can no longer, in the light of reason which he holds dear, assert that "there is no God."

The soul-winner can move rapidly to show the doubter what the Bible declares about the existence of a living God. The Bible shows how nature declares God (Psalm 19:1–2). Other classic Scriptures to set forth the Bible teaching about God are: Romans 1:19–22; Genesis 1:1; Genesis 17:1; Joshua 24:19; Nahum 1:2; Psalm 139:1–6; Jeremiah 23:23; Romans 1:23; 1 Corinthians 10:13; John 4:24; Hebrews 12:29; 1 John 4:8,16.

Explain to him the plan of salvation. It is necessary to review it again and again as you deal with the skeptic. This is true with almost any type of person with whom you deal.

(1) All have sinned (1 John 1:8–10).

(2) Therefore, all are under the wrath of God (John 3:36).

(3) God has provided an escape through the death of Christ (Rom. 5:6).

(4) The penalty for sin falls on the sinless Christ and not upon the guilty (Gal. 3:13).

(5) If any will believe God's testimony, he has everlasting life (John 5:24).

(6) If you receive the witness of men, why not receive the witness of God? (1 John 5:9–12).

Chapter 12

How to Deal with False Hopes

A surprisingly large number of people have rested themselves in some type of false hope. They are trusting something besides Jesus for soul salvation. Some are depending on a system, while others trust in some type of feeling. Many have found hope in some notion which grows out of a misunderstanding of certain basic truths. To reach these people, it is necessary to break down their false hopes and to help them realize that there is but one hope. Help them to see that hope is in Christ and not in notions, systems, or feelings.

We shall deal with only the most prevalent false hopes.

"God Is Too Good to Damn Anyone"

This false hope is possibly the most prominent of this group. It is generally the result of faulty preaching. It is often bred by the preaching which declares that "it is not possible to harmonize the spirit of Jesus with the damnation of sinners."

This false hope depends on a negative. It presumes on the goodness of God. It is not in harmony with the specific teachings of Jesus. Jesus said, "He that believeth on the Son hath everlasting life: and he that believeth not the Son shall not see life; but the wrath of God abideth on him" (John 3:36). Again Jesus taught, saying, "Marvel not at this: for the hour is coming, in the which all that are in the graves shall hear his voice, and

143

shall come forth; they that have done good, unto the resurrection of life; and they that have done evil, unto the resurrection of damnation" (John 5:28–29). Jesus in this teaching definitely declares that both the good and the evil man shall be raised from the dead and that the evil shall be raised unto damnation.

Whatever Jesus did and taught must be and is in keeping with his Spirit. He knew sin would damn and that lost men were under just condemnation, and he has done everything in his power to warn the sinner and to save him. He died on the cross for the sinner. He gave many of the plain warnings and instructions found in the Bible for their guidance. He did more. He has sent the Holy Spirit to convict of sin and has established churches as lighthouses in the earth. It appears, therefore, to the writer that there is no contradiction between the spirit of Christ and the destruction of men who will not hear and who wilfully rebel against God.

How to Deal with This Kind of False Hope

Point up that God does not damn sinners. Tell him that sin damns. Go a step further and help him see that sin damns him with his own consent. "Ye will not come to me, that ye might have life" (John 5:40). Read this verse to him, and show him that it places the responsibility for his destruction on the sinner and not on God. It says, "Ye will not come to me." God has provided a way of escape, but the sinner must accept the way. Show him that his unwillingness to accept God's provision places the responsibility on him and not on God. His statement does not challenge the goodness of God, but rather it indicates an unwillingness to accept God's goodness. The goodness of God must be accepted, and that is the privilege of the sinner. To say instead that God is too good to damn a sinner is to hide behind a negation rather than openly to accept a positive solution.

Show the victim of this false hope that God has no pleasure in the death of the wicked (Ezek. 33:11). All who go to hell go there against the will of God. They also go there despite all of

God's effort to prevent it. God has done many things to reach the sinner. He gave his Son to die on the cross. He sent the blessed Holy Spirit to convict and guide (John 16:13; Acts 1:8). He gave the churches and preachers to warn and instruct. He has sent into the earth thousands of soul-winners who have a sense of their mission and who really care. God has done all possible to arrest the attention of the victim of this false hope and bring him to salvation. If he persists in his false security, he will be eternally lost.

Show him the destiny of the victims of this false hope. "If God spared not the angels that sinned, but cast them down to hell, and delivered them into chains of darkness, to be reserved unto judgment; and spared not the old world, . . . and turning the cities of Sodom and Gomorrha into ashes . . ." (2 Peter 2:4–6). Ask him, "Who are we to presume on the goodness of God?" If God spared not these ancient people from his judgment, who are we to presume on the patience and justice of God? If one says that God is too good to damn a sinner, let him find out what God will do, not by speculation, but by reading God's Word and history. What happened to the angels who sinned? They were delivered into chains of darkness (2 Peter 2:4). What happened to the generation of Noah who presumed on God's goodness? God sent a flood to destroy them (2 Peter 2:5). What became of the wicked cities of the day of Lot? God turned them into ashes (2 Peter 2:6). God did not leave us to speculate about the destiny of those who choose some other way of salvation than Jesus himself. He has told us plainly their awful fate.

Show him that God is the God of justice. The victim of this false hope makes much of the goodness of God. Lead him to recognize that the goodness of God is inseparably tied up with justice. There is no goodness apart from justice. If God is good, he must be just. If he is just, he must require a payment for all sin. He must see that all injustice be rectified. Either the sinner must pay for his sins, or someone in position to do so must pay for his sins. They cannot be overlooked. "For the wages of sin is death; but the gift of God is eternal life through Jesus Christ our Lord" (Rom. 6:23). The only escape from the wages of sin is a gift from God, and that gift is eternal life through Jesus Christ and not some false notion or negation.

When you have unhinged him from his false hope, give him the simple plan of salvation.

"I Feel All Right"

We do not say that there are no feelings connected with wonderful redemption, because men are emotional as well as intellectual and volitional. It must be thoroughly understood, however, that nowhere in the Bible is it taught that feeling is a trustworthy evidence of salvation. A sense of the presence of God and a deep spiritual satisfaction come along with redemption generally, but not as an evidence of salvation. It is one of the joys and rewards of being properly related to God. God never intended that feeling be a proof of our relation to him, because so many things may affect one's feelings. Overeating, a sick body, a keen disappointment in some person may affect one's feelings. We cannot always depend on our feelings, but we can depend on God.

How to Deal with This False Hope

Help the confused to see that it is not what "seems" that matters. Point up that he may feel all right because he has not given the Holy Spirit a chance to enlighten him. A man may drive his car at sixty miles per hour down a road, oblivious that around the next curve a bridge has been washed out. He will feel all right as he heads right into certain death. He feels all right only because he is ignorant of the facts. If someone stops him and acquaints him with the facts, he will stop and turn back. This is the case of one who feels all right only because he does not know the facts. Ask him why he feels all right. Ask him if he has any Bible fact on which to base his feeling of security. Point up to him that "there is a way which seemeth right unto a man, but the end thereof are the ways of death" (Prov. 14:12).

Lead him to see that there is a difference between a faith that depends on feeling and faith that rests on the Word of God.[1] Teach him to trust God. Teach him that if he simply takes God at his word, he will be saved whether any feeling accompanies his experience or not. Show him the difference in a feeling of false security and one based on the unshakable Word of God. Read to him, "For God so loved the world, that he gave his only begotten Son, that whosoever believeth in him should not perish, but have everlasting life" (John 3:16). Tell him that if he will trust in Jesus he will receive everlasting life. Ask him if he believes that God will keep his word. If his answer is yes, then urge him to depend on God's Word rather than feelings. Point up that Paul had hope of eternal life, but that he built his hope on the Word of God and not on his feelings (Titus 1:2).

Show him that Jesus is the only way. "Jesus saith unto him, I am the way, the truth, and the life: no man cometh unto the Father, but by me" (John 14:6). Again, Jesus said, "I am the door: by me if any man enter in, he shall be saved, and shall go in and out, and find pasture" (John 10:9).

Dependence upon Religion for Salvation

There is a difference in being religious and in being a Christian. Religion is a way of saving oneself by employing good deeds. The nature of this hope is religious and not spiritual, is of man and not of God. Christianity is spiritual. The good deeds on which this type of false hope depends consist of church membership, church attendance, contributions, and church work. Religiosity is substituted for regeneration. One substitutes church relations for a proper relation with God.

How to Win This Kind of Person

He must be properly related to God. Many of these people are church members, but they are not children of God. Show him that one becomes a child of God through the new birth. Nicodemus was a deeply religious man, but Jesus did not give him any credit for that on his salvation. Jesus told him plainly, "Marvel not that I said unto thee, Ye must be born again" (John 3:7). Paul was clear on this point when he taught, "Not by works of righteousness which we have done, but according to his mercy he saved us, by the washing of regeneration, and renewing of the Holy Ghost" (Titus 3:5). Paul said in another place, "Therefore if any man be in Christ, he is a new creature [creation]" (2 Cor. 5:17). One, therefore, becomes a child of God by birth into God's family. The new relation to God is the determining factor in salvation (Rom. 8:16–17). A personal, transforming experience with God, and not church work, makes one a Christian. Christianity is a way of life, and it *is* life. It is the life of God in us. Good deeds and church work are the natural results of Christianity, but not the way to become a Christian. One works for God because he is a Christian and not in order to win life eternal.

Show the religious person how to receive salvation. Use Cornelius as a Bible example of how a religious man became dissatisfied with religion and looked to God for something real. Cornelius did everything that the average church member performs. He feared God (Acts 10:2). He was a devout man (v. 2). He made fabulous contributions (v. 2). He even prayed to God (v. 2). The Bible described him as a just man (v. 22). With all this to his credit, Cornelius knew that he was not saved. He knew that he lacked something. An angel appeared unto him in a vision and told him, "And now send men to Joppa, and call for one Simon, . . . he shall tell thee what thou oughtest to do" (Acts 10:5–6). Peter came to Caesarea and entered the house of Cornelius and preached to him and his household. There are three things here which should be presented to the religious person.

First, Peter preached, "To him give all the prophets witness, that through his name whosoever believeth in him shall receive remission of sins" (Acts 10:43). Peter urged Cornelius to believe in the name of Jesus. Later, when Peter reported the incident to the brethren in Jerusalem, he said, "When they heard these things, they held their peace, and glorified God, saying, Then hath God also to the Gentiles granted repentance unto life" (Acts 11:18).

Here we see that Peter explained to Cornelius that he must repent. The account tells us also that "while Peter yet spake these words, the Holy Ghost fell on all them which heard the word. . . . And he commanded them to be baptized in the name of the Lord" (Acts 10:44–48).

We also learn from this account that when they believed and repented, the Spirit fell on them, and they were saved. The New Testament tells us that the good, religious life of Cornelius was not enough and that when he heard the gospel he believed, repented, and was washed clean by the Holy Ghost, and was baptized.

Chapter 13

How to Deal with the Fearful

Fear is man's chief enemy. Fear breeds worry and confusion. Worry kills more people than all the deadly microbes combined. Fear leads to jealousy. Fear is back of international mistrust and leads to great armament programs. Fear has wrought havoc in every field of human life. In the realm of the spiritual, however, fear has done its worst. If Satan can eclipse one with fear, he will contain him in a sphere of suspended anguish which will prevent him from contact with hope. Many a man has failed in business because he was too fearful to explore the possibilities around him. More, however, have died in their sins because of fears of personal consequences or of self. We shall discuss the three most prevalent fears.

Fear that One Has Committed the Unpardonable Sin

"I have committed the unpardonable sin" is the cry of deep despair. Almost all who say this are only victims of a fear complex. Often this complex is created by preachers who are so anxious to see folks saved that they misrepresent the truth. More often it is the cumulative effect of many guilt complexes.

How to Deal with the Person with This Fear

Ask him what he thinks the unpardonable sin is. His answer will reveal that he is not guilty of the unpardonable sin. He may
150

say that he resisted the Holy Spirit until he took his flight. To resist the Holy Spirit is a dangerous and dreadful thing, but help him to see that it is not the unpardonable sin. All have resisted the Holy Spirit, and anyone who persists in it will be lost because of his unbelief. But if one repents and turns to Christ, he will be saved. The unpardonable sin is something that one can never get forgiveness for from the time of the act.

Show him what the unpardonable sin is. Jesus gave the definition of the unpardonable sin and then explained it.

The background against which the sin is committed.—Jesus healed a demoniac and many other sick people and was very popular with the crowds. The Pharisees were jealous of him. They tried to discredit him with the people. To do this, they did not deny the mighty deeds of Jesus but impugned them by accusing him of being in collusion with Satan. Jesus clarified the issue by saying, "And if Satan cast out Satan, he is divided against himself; . . . And if I by Beelzebub cast out devils, . . . But if I cast out devils by the Spirit of God, then the kingdom of God is come unto you" (Matt. 12:26-28). The issue was, In what power did Jesus perform his works? If he did them in the power of the Holy Ghost, then the kingdom of God had come. The religionists did not want to admit this, and to avoid it, they charged Jesus with working in the power of Satan. This was a wilful speaking against the Holy Spirit out of a heart of jealousy. This is the background against which Jesus defined the unpardonable sin.

The definition of the sin.—Jesus defined it in these words: "Wherefore I say unto you, All manner of sin and blasphemy shall be forgiven unto men: but the blasphemy against the Holy Ghost shall not be forgiven unto men" (Matt. 12:31). From this definition we learn that the unpardonable sin is blasphemy. It is a sin of the tongue. It is, therefore, a sin of the speech. It is blasphemy against the Holy Spirit. It is not rejecting Jesus, nor is it a series of stubborn resistances of the Holy Spirit. It is a sin of the speech.

The definition explained.—Jesus gave the definition. Then he followed the definition with a brief but thorough explanation. "And whosoever speaketh a word against the Son of man, it shall be forgiven him: but whosoever speaketh against the Holy Ghost, it shall not be forgiven him, neither in this world, neither in the world to come" (Matt. 12:32). The unpardonable sin is to blaspheme the Holy Ghost. But what is blasphemy? Here Jesus says, "But whosoever speaketh against the Holy Ghost. . . ." It is, therefore, to speak against the Holy Ghost. The content of the speech is to attribute the works of Christ to the devil rather than to the Holy Ghost. The motive was religious jealousy. The purpose was to cast reflection on Jesus and frighten the crowds away from him.

When you have explained this to the fearful, ask him, "Have you done this?" He will answer no. Then point up to him again that he is therefore not guilty of the sin.

In further clarification, ask him certain questions. Ask him, "Why are you concerned about your condition?" Ask him, "Why did you come to church today?" Then show him that if he had committed the unpardonable sin, he would not be concerned and would never go to church again. Show him that only the Holy Spirit can convict of sin and create concern (John 16:8–11). "No man can come to me, except the Father which hath sent me draw him" (John 6:44). Help him to see that the Spirit of God is still striving with him, or he would have no concern for himself and no inclination to come to church.

Encourage him by showing him that he is closer to salvation than he thinks. He has the advantage over the majority of sinners. He knows he is a sinner. He realizes that he is a great sinner. Help him to see that this is to his advantage. Help him to see that Christ died for all sinners. He died to save great sinners. "This is a faithful saying, and worthy of all acceptation, that Christ Jesus came into the world to save sinners; of whom I am chief" (1 Tim. 1:15). Show him that Jesus can save blasphemers. "Who was before a blasphemer, and a persecutor, and injurious: but I obtained mercy, because I did it ignorantly in unbelief" (1 Tim. 1:13).

Explain the simple plan of salvation to him. Then give great emphasis to the ability of Jesus. "Wherefore he is able also to save them to the uttermost that come unto God by him, seeing he ever liveth to make intercession for them" (Heb. 7:25). Show him that Jesus is "able to save them to the uttermost." Place mighty emphasis on "able" and "uttermost." One describes the limitless ability of Jesus, and the other the worst state of a sinner. Christ's ability can reach the uttermost. That means that any anxious sinner can be saved.

Fear of Personal Consequences

There are two types of personal fears:

There is the person who fears the loss of friends and business. Help this person to see that his soul is of more value than things. "For what is a man profited, if he shall gain the whole world, and lose his own soul?" (Matt. 16:26). Explain that fear like this is often ungrounded. The devil tries to use the prospects of the loss of business and friends to frighten one away from soul salvation. When his fears are without cause, use this argument. But in many instances this fear is real. When the fear is real, help him realize that the loss of his soul is a greater tragedy than the loss of his business or of his so-called friends.

Show him that the wisdom of the ages is on the side of the man who trusts God. "The fear of man bringeth a snare: but whoso putteth his trust in the Lord shall be safe" (Prov. 29:25). If he persists in his present position, he will fall into an inevitable trap of sin; but if he dares to trust in the Lord, he will be secure. Point out that if he chooses the friendship of fools over the salvation of God, he will be destroyed (Prov. 13:20).

Then there is the individual who fears criticism and persecution. Do not deny that he might be persecuted and ridiculed. Show him that other Christians before him have been persecuted. Jesus and his disciples were persecuted. "The disciple is not above his master, nor the servant above his lord. It is enough for the disciple that he be as his master, and the servant as his lord. If they have called the master of the house Beelzebub, how much more shall they call them of his household? Fear them not therefore" (Matt. 10:24–26).

Point up the reward of the persecuted. "Blessed are ye, when men shall . . . persecute you, . . . for great is your reward in heaven: for so persecuted they the prophets which were before you" (Matt. 5:11–12). The reward of the persecuted is threefold:

(1) The persecuted shall have glories in heaven (Rom. 8:18).

(2) The persecuted shall be associated in life, death, and eternity with the mighty prophets and kingdom-builders of history (Matt. 5:12).

(3) He will even be prosperous here in this life (Mark 10:29–30). It is safer and better to stand on the promises of God and receive his sure prosperity than to receive the applause of worldly fanatics.

Fear of Self

This fear strikes in two directions:

First, there is the fear of the power of sin in one's life. This person is generally dominated by some great sin, like adultery or gambling.

Show that the power of sin is broken in one's life by Christ. "If the Son therefore shall make you free, ye shall be free indeed" (John 8:36). Often the fearful has resolved to quit his sins, but has fallen immediately back into the grip of sin. This honest effort to throw off the yoke of sin in one's own strength failed and resulted in despair. The soul-winner, therefore, must help him to see that his intentions were correct but his method was wrong. He tried to overcome sin in his own power, whereas he should have done it in the power of Christ. He must see that men are made free from sin only in Christ. Get him to try once again, only this time let Jesus break the power of sin in his life. If he is interested, then tell him how it is done. Tell him that he must come to God through faith in Christ and repentance toward God.

Explain to him that Christ has saved great numbers of people who were fully as bad as, if not worse than, himself (John 4:17–30; 8:1–11; etc.).

Help him to realize that Christ can save men unto the uttermost (Heb. 7:25).

Get him to see that he must desire deliverance from his sins. He must co-operate in doing two things: (1) Turn against the reign of sin in his body (Rom. 6:12). (2) Yield to God rather than to the instruments of unrighteousness (Rom. 6:13).

This type of fearful is only conscious of his weakness. This is in some respects in his favor. The sinner must realize that he is a guilty sinner and that he is too weak to redeem himself. However, this person's trouble is that he knows only of his own weakness. He has no knowledge of any positive strength which is able to match his weakness.

The soul-winner will immediately agree that the fearful person is weak. He will admit that he cannot hold out against Satan in his own strength.

Show the fearful that he is saved and kept by the strength of Christ. When Christ becomes his Saviour, he receives several powerful allies which the sinner standing alone does not have.

(1) He will have Christ the Saviour to stand by him.

(2) He will be given a new nature, and will no longer love sin (2 Cor. 5:17).

(3) The Holy Spirit will be present to guide and empower him (Rom. 8:16; 1 Cor. 2:10; Acts 1:8).

With powerful allies like these the individual cannot be defeated by Satan. If the fearful receives the proper amount of encouragement from these statements, then from this point one will proceed to teach him step by step what a Christian is and how to become a Christian.

Notes

Chapter 1: Individual Evangelism

1. A. C. Archibald, *New Testament Evangelism* (Philadelphia: Judson Press, 1946), p. 44.
2. Charles G. Trumbull, *Taking Men Alive* (New York: Young Men's Christian Association Press, 1908), p. 32.
3. *Ibid.*, p. 34.
4. *Newsweek*, May 28, 1948, p. 84.
5. Percy O. Ruoff, *Personal Work* (London: Inter-Varsity Fellowship, 1946), p. 12.
6. J. W. Chapman, *Fishing for Men* (Chicago: Winona Publishing Co., 1904), p. 72.
7. E. Y. Mullins, *Talks on Soul-Winning* (Nashville: The Sunday School Board of the Southern Baptist Convention, 1920), p. 9.

Chapter 2: The Qualifications of the Soul-Winner

1. R. A. Torrey, *How to Work for Christ* (Los Angeles: Fleming H. Revell Co., n.d.), p. 14.
2. E. Myers Harrison and Walter L. Wilson, *How to Win Souls* (Wheaton: Van Kampen Press, 1952), p. 11.
3. J. C. Macaulay and Robert H. Belton, *Personal Evangelism* (Chicago: Moody Press, 1956), p. 71.
4. C. H. Spurgeon, *The Soul-Winner* (New York: Fleming H. Revell Co., 1895), p. 40.
5. *Ibid.*, p. 41.
6. Torrey, *op. cit.*, p. 17.
7. Macaulay, *op. cit.*, p. 82.
8. Harrison and Wilson, *op. cit.*, p. 18.

Chapter 3: The Equipment of the Soul-Winner

1. Oscar Lowry, *Scripture Memorizing for Successful Soul-Winning* (Grand Rapids: Zondervan Publishing House), p. 15.
2. Trumbull, *op. cit.*, pp. 115 ff.
3. W. E. Sangster, *Let Me Commend* (Nashville: Abingdon-Cokesbury Press, 1948), p. 16.
4. Mullins, *op. cit.*, p. 16.
5. *Ibid.*, p. 17.
6. David M. Dawson, *More Power in Soul-Winning* (Grand Rapids: Zondervan Publishing House), p. 37.
7. Ruoff, *op. cit.*, p. 29.

Chapter 4: The Approach

1. George E. Sweazey, *Effective Evangelism* (New York: Harper & Brothers Publishers, 1953), p. 58.
2. A. W. Knox, *Personal Evangelism* (Minneapolis: The Lutheran Bible Institute, 1934), p. 70.
3. Ruoff, *op. cit.*, p. 48.
4. Sweazey, *op. cit.*, p. 58.
5. Chester Wilkins, Jr., *A Handbook for Personal Soul-Winning* (Berne, Indiana: Light and Hope Publications, 1950), p. 63.
6. *Ibid.*, p. 62.
7. Gaines S. Dobbins, *Evangelism According to Christ* (Nashville: Broadman Press, 1949), p. 37.
8. Henry C. Mabie, *Method in Soul-Winning* (Chicago: Fleming H. Revell Co., 1906), pp. 86 ff.
9. Edward Hastings, *The Speaker's Bible*, "The Gospel According to St. John" (Aberdeen, Scotland: The Speaker's Bible Office, 1931), Vol. III, p. 38.
10. Walter L. Wilson, *Let's Go Fishing With the Doctor* (Findlay, Ohio: Fundamental Truth Publications, 1936), p. 17.
11. Knox, *op. cit.*, p. 62.
12. Sweazey, *op. cit.*, p. 58.

Chapter 5: Techniques of the Master Soul-Winner

1. Clarence E. Macartney, *Great Interviews of Jesus* (Nashville: Abingdon-Cokesbury Press, 1944), p. 28.
2. Raymond Calkins, *How Jesus Dealt With Men* (Nashville: Abingdon-Cokesbury Press, 1942), p. 55.

3. Macartney, *op. cit.*, p. 28.
4. L. R. Scarborough, *How Jesus Won Men* (Nashville: Sunday School Board of the Southern Baptist Convention, 1926), p. 80.
5. F. V. McFatridge, *The Personal Evangelism of Jesus* (Grand Rapids: Zondervan Publishing House, 1939), p. 43.
6. Macartney, *op. cit.*, p. 30.
7. Calkins, *op. cit.*, p. 64.
8. Scarborough, *op. cit.*, p. 82.
9. Walter Barlow, *God So Loved* (London: Fleming H. Revell Co., 1952), p. 46.
10. Matthew Henry, *Commentary on the Whole Bible* (New York: Fleming H. Revell Co., 1721), Vol. V.

Chapter 6: How to Win the Anxious

1. Calkins, *op. cit.*, p. 41.
2. Scarborough, *op. cit.*, p. 60.
3. Torrey, *op. cit.*, p. 37.
4. Knox, *op. cit.*, p. 113.

Chapter 7: How to Win the Indifferent

1. *Ibid.*, p. 95.
2. M. W. Downey, *The Art of Soul-Winning* (Grand Rapids: Baker Book House, 1957), p. 83.
3. William W. Frank in collaboration with Charles L. Lapp, *How to Outsell the Born Salesman* (New York: The Macmillan Co., 1959), p. 12.
4. *Ibid.*, p. 13.
5. Torrey, *op. cit.*, p. 52.
6. William Evans, *Personal Soul-Winning* (Chicago: The Bible Institute Colportage Association, 1910), p. 59.
7. Torrey, *op. cit.*, p. 44.
8. Harrison and Wilson, *op. cit.*, p. 70.
9. Knox, *op. cit.*, p. 99.
10. Percy H. Whiting, *The Five Great Rules of Selling* (New York: McGraw-Hill Book Co., Inc., 1957), p. 181.
11. *Ibid.*, p. 185.

Chapter 8: How to Win the Jewish People

1. Arthur W. Kac, *The Rebirth of the State of Israel* (Chicago: Moody Press, 1958), p. 116.

2. Jase Jones from a lecture delivered in the classroom of Evangelism at Southwestern Baptist Theological Seminary, Fort Worth, Texas, December 8, 1959.

3. *Ibid.*

4. Joseph Zeitlin, *Disciples of The Wise* (New York: Teachers College, Columbia University, 1947), p. 76.

5. Kac, *op. cit.*, p. 95.

6. Targum is the Aramaic translation and interpretation of the Old Testament.

7. Kac, *op. cit.*, p. 215.

8. Alfred Edersheim, *The Life and Times of Jesus the Messiah* (New York: Longmans, Green and Company, 8th Edition, 1899), Vol. 2, App. IX.

9. Kac, *op. cit.*, p. 218.

10. *Ibid.*, p. 220.

11. David Baron, *The Servant of Jehovah* (London: Morgan & Scott, 2nd Edition, 1922), p. 11.

12. Leroy Gager, *Handbook for Soul-Winners* (Grand Rapids: Zondervan Publishing House, 1956), p. 139.

13. *Ibid.*, p. 139.

14. Macaulay and Belton, *op. cit.*, p. 228.

Chapter 9: How to Win the Catholics

1. Harrison and Wilson, *op. cit.*, p. 111.

2. Rev. Francis Spirago and Richard F. Clarke, *The Catechism Explained* (Cincinnati: Benziger Bros. Corp., 1927), p. 125.

3. *Ibid.*, p. 465.

4. *Ibid.*, p. 470.

5. *Ibid.*, p. 572.

6. *Ibid.*, p. 573.

7. *Ibid.*, p. 582.

8. Harrison and Wilson, *op. cit.*, p. 113.

9. Spirago and Clarke, *op. cit.*, p. 594.

10. Harrison and Wilson, *op. cit.*, p. 118.

11. Gager, *op. cit.*, p. 172.

Chapter 10: How to Win the Spiritists

1. Jan Karel Van Baalen, *The Chaos of Cults* (Grand Rapids: Wm. B. Eerdmans Publishing Company, 1955), p. 21.

2. W. H. Larrabee, *The New Schaff-Herzog* Encyclopedia (New York: Funk and Wagnalls Co., 1911), Vol. XI, p. 51.

3. Van Baalen, *op. cit.*, p. 22.
4. *Ibid.*, p. 43.
5. Harrison and Wilson, *op. cit.*, p. 125.
6. R. B. Jones, *Spiritism in Bible Light* (London: 1921), p. 172.
7. A. Conan Doyle, *The New Revelation* (New York: 1918).
8. Jones, *op. cit.*, p. 172.
9. Van Baalen, *op. cit.*, p. 23.
10. *Ibid.*, p. 39.

Chapter 11: How to Win the Doubters

1. L. R. Scarborough, *With Christ After the Lost* (Nashville: Broadman Press, 1952), p. 187.
2. Torrey, *op. cit.*, p. 117.
3. Harrison and Wilson, *op. cit.*, p. 83.

Chapter 12: How to Deal with False Hopes

1. Torrey, *op. cit.*, p. 100.